Better Homes and Gardens®

MENU
COOK BOOK

Delight your family or guests with this New Orleans-style Creole Jambalaya, a dish that teams ham with shrimp, rice, vegetables, and seasonings. (Recipe on page 69.)

On the cover: Onion slices garnish Home-Style Round Steak. Also shown are Saucy Succotash, Fresh Vegetable Platter, and Berry Cheesecake Pie. (Recipes on page 26.)

BETTER HOMES AND GARDENS BOOKS

Editorial Director: Don Dooley
Managing Editor: Malcolm E. Robinson   Art Director: John Berg
Food Editor: Nancy Morton
Senior Food Editor: Joyce Trollope
Associate Editors: Rosemary Corsiglia, Sharyl Heiken, Rosalie Riglin
Assistant Editors: Sandra Mosley, Sandra Mapes,
Elizabeth Strait
Copy Editor: Lawrence Clayton
Designers: Harijs Priekulis, Tonya Rodriguez

CONTENTS

Our seal assures you that every recipe in the *Menu Cook Book* is endorsed by the Better Homes and Gardens Test Kitchen. Each recipe has been tested for family appeal, practicality, and deliciousness.

MAKING MENUS WORK

Do you want to serve meals that are attractive, tasty, and nutritious—meals that have plenty of flavor variety, yet still fit into the family's busy schedules? The menus in this book are designed to help you accomplish this, both for family meals and when entertaining. Each menu is practical and consists of favorite foods, interestingly combined, that look and taste good together. All use the Basic Four Food Groups as a nutritional yardstick.

Basic Four Food Groups: Nutritionists, to provide a handy guide to serving nutritious meals, have divided foods into four classifications—Meat, Vegetable-Fruit, Bread-Cereal, and Milk. Although most foods contain combinations of vitamins, minerals, proteins, carbohydrates, or fats, the groupings reflect important sources of key nutrients. A diet that supplies adequate amounts of these key nutrients will include the other things needed.

Meat Group—Protein-rich foods such as meat, poultry, eggs, fish, dry beans, lentils, nuts, and peanut butter are in this group. Each person needs 2 or more servings from this group per day. For example, 2 or 3 ounces boneless, lean, cooked meat counts as 1 meat serving as do 2 eggs, 1 cup cooked dry beans, or 4 tablespoons peanut butter. (Check this portion size against what you normally serve to see if your meat servings are generous or skimpy.)

Vegetable-Fruit Group—Assorted minerals and vitamins, especially vitamins A and C, are the key nutrients in fresh, canned, or frozen produce. Plan 4 or more servings from this group every day. Include 1 source of vitamin C daily and 1 of vitamin A every other day. Citrus fruits, plus cantaloupe, strawberries, green

peppers, and Brussels sprouts are good sources of vitamin C. Dark green and deep yellow vegetables and fruits are high in vitamin A. Use other vegetables and fruits for variety and to fulfill Basic Four Food requirements.

Count 1/2 cup cooked or sliced foods or the portion normally served such as 1 apple or half a grapefruit as 1 vegetable-fruit serving.

Bread-Cereal Group—The B vitamins and several minerals are the contribution of the whole grain, enriched, or restored cereals and baked products in this group. Plan on 4 or more servings daily, using 1 slice bread, 1 ounce ready-to-eat cereal, or 1/2 to 3/4 cup cooked cereal, grits, noodles, or rice as 1 serving.

Milk Group—Everyone needs the calcium, phosphorus, and other body-building nutrients in milk daily. Adults need two 8-ounce cups, while children need 3 to 4 cups, depending upon age. Pregnant women need 3 or more cups and nursing mothers at least 4 cups.

Various dairy products can be substituted for part of the milk servings. For example, 1 ounce Cheddar cheese equals 1/2 serving milk, while 1/2 cup cottage cheese or 1/2 cup of ice cream replaces 1/3 and 1/4 milk servings respectively. (The cheeses also contribute protein to the diet but are placed in the milk group because of their calcium content. You can count 2 ounces Cheddar or 1/2 cup cottage cheese as 1 meat serving, if desired.)

To Use Menus in Daily Meal Plan:

1. Select one of the dinner menus. Make a note of Basic Four Food Value of the menu.

2. Figure the Basic Four Food Value of breakfast next. Use one of these menus or your own version of the fruit, bread or cereal, milk, and egg or meat breakfast pattern.

3. Allocate the remaining Basic Four Foods to lunch. Meals carried or eaten at home are easy to figure. (The person eating out should try to fit his choices to the day's plan.)

4. Repeat the three steps until several days are planned. Use the chapter on leftovers or substitute vegetable recipes as needed.

A sophisticated supper

← For buffet entertaining, feature *Steaks Bertrand* and a tossed salad with *Creamy Garlic Dressing*. (Recipes on page 54.)

Menus for Everyday Meals

Corned beef special

Family-Style Dinner features *Glazed Corned Beef* surrounded by spiced peaches and cherry tomatoes. Replace the traditional cabbage with *Cauliflower with Cheese Sauce* and a pleasantly zippy *Hot Bean Salad* made with Italian green beans, onions, and herbs. Then, bake a fragrant loaf of *Anadama Bread*, that New England specialty made from cornmeal and molasses. (Recipes on page 29.)

Match the menus in this chapter to your family's food likes, time schedules, and nutritional needs. You can combine a breakfast menu and a lunch with the dinner menu of your choice, but be sure that the ingredients in the day's menus meet the Basic Four Food Groups' daily requirements. Included are menus that contain recipes for oven meals, make-ahead dishes, and dishes cooked on an outdoor grill.

MORNING MEALS

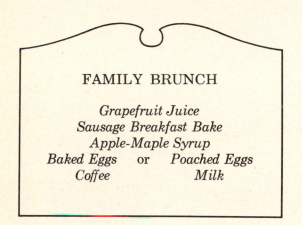

FAMILY BRUNCH

Grapefruit Juice
Sausage Breakfast Bake
Apple-Maple Syrup
Baked Eggs or *Poached Eggs*
Coffee *Milk*

Basic Four Food Value of Menu (see page 5): 1 serving meat, 1½ servings vegetable-fruit, 1 serving bread-cereal, and 1 serving milk.

Special Helps: Eliminate the time-consuming steps of frying bacon or sausage, cooking eggs, and making toast by baking all the breakfast together in the oven. Just prepare the Sausage Breakfast Bake and put it into the oven. Then, make the Apple-Maple Syrup, break the eggs into custard cups, and set the table. Put the eggs into the oven 10 minutes after the Sausage Breakfast Bake has begun cooking so they will finish baking at the same time. Now, you have about 25 minutes to dress, read the paper, or do other tasks before serving breakfast to the family.

BAKED EGGS

    6 eggs
      Salt
      Pepper
    6 teaspoons milk

Butter 6 custard cups. Break one egg into each cup; sprinkle with salt and pepper. To each egg, add 1 teaspoon of the milk. Set cups in a shallow baking pan; pour hot water into the pan to depth of 1 inch. Bake at 350° till eggs are firm, about 25 minutes. Makes 6 servings.

SAUSAGE BREAKFAST BAKE

    2 cups packaged pancake mix
 1¼ cups milk
    2 eggs
    2 tablespoons salad oil
    1 14-ounce jar spiced apple rings
    1 8-ounce package brown-and-serve
      sausage links

Combine pancake mix, milk, eggs, and salad oil; beat till nearly smooth with rotary beater. Turn into a greased 13½x8¾x1¾-inch baking dish. Drain apple rings, reserving the syrup to use in the Apple-Maple Syrup. Halve each sausage link crosswise. Arrange apple rings and sausages atop batter in a pattern so the mixture can be cut into squares when baked. Bake at 350° till done, about 30 to 35 minutes. Cut into 6 squares. Serve with Apple-Maple Syrup. Makes 6 servings.

APPLE-MAPLE SYRUP

      Spiced apple syrup
   ⅓ cup sugar
    4 teaspoons cornstarch
    1 tablespoon butter or margarine
   ¾ cup maple-flavored syrup

Add water to reserved spiced apple syrup from Sausage Breakfast Bake to equal ⅔ cup. In saucepan combine sugar and cornstarch; stir in spiced apple syrup. Cook and stir till thick and bubbly; cook and stir 1 minute more. Stir in butter and maple syrup. Serve over Sausage Breakfast Bake. Makes 1½ cups syrup.

Cheerful beginning for the day

Drizzle *Apple-Maple Syrup* over squares of →
Sausage Breakfast Bake for a breakfast treat that's sure to wake up appetites.

WEEKEND BREAKFAST

Melon Appetizer
Canadian-Style Bacon
Double Corn Waffles or Banana Waffles
Hot Maple Syrup   Butter
Coffee   Milk

Basic Four Food Value of Menu (see page 5) : ½ serving meat, 1 serving vegetable-fruit, 1 serving bread-cereal, and 1 serving milk.

Special Helps: Weekends allow more time to prepare and serve a leisurely breakfast. Take advantage of this extra time to make waffles. For a variation of the standard recipe, choose either the Double Corn Waffles or the Banana Waffles. If you are preparing Banana Waffles, enlist the help of an electric blender to speed up mixing and to eliminate mashing bananas by hand. Place the liquid ingredients (egg, milk, and salad oil) in the blender first and blend till they are mixed. Add the dry ingredients and the banana, cut in chunks. Blend just till all of the ingredients are combined and the banana is mashed. Bake as directed in recipe.

MELON APPETIZER

Another time try green grapes in place of the honeydew balls for a different combination—

    2 cups cantaloupe balls or cubes
    2 cups honeydew balls or cubes
    1 cup orange juice
    1 tablespoon lemon juice
        • • •
        Confectioners' sugar

Combine melon balls or cubes. Mix orange juice and lemon juice together; pour over melon balls. Chill overnight. Ladle melons and juice into 6 serving dishes; sprinkle generously with confectioners' sugar. Makes 6 servings.

DOUBLE CORN WAFFLES

    1 cup sifted all-purpose flour
    2 teaspoons baking powder
    1 teaspoon baking soda
    1 teaspoon sugar
    ½ teaspoon salt
    1 cup yellow cornmeal
    2 beaten egg yolks
    1½ cups buttermilk
    ¼ cup salad oil
    1 8¾-ounce can cream-style corn
    2 stiffly beaten egg whites

Sift together the first 5 ingredients; stir in cornmeal. Combine egg yolks, buttermilk, and salad oil; add to dry ingredients. Stir in corn. Fold in egg whites. Bake in preheated waffle baker. Makes three 10-inch waffles.

BANANA WAFFLES

    2¼ cups sifted all-purpose flour
    4 teaspoons baking powder
    1½ tablespoons sugar
    ¾ teaspoon salt
    2 beaten eggs
    1¾ cups milk
    ¾ cup mashed banana (1 banana)
    ½ cup salad oil

Sift together first 4 ingredients. Mix together eggs, milk, banana, and oil till blended. Add banana mixture to dry ingredients, stirring only till moistened. Pour *one-third* of the batter onto preheated waffle baker. Bake till brown, about 5 minutes. Repeat with remaining batter. Makes three 10-inch waffles.

HOT MAPLE SYRUP

    1 cup light corn syrup
    ½ cup brown sugar
        Dash maple flavoring
    1 tablespoon butter or margarine

Mix corn syrup, sugar, and ½ cup water. Cook and stir till sugar is dissolved. Add maple flavoring and butter. Makes 2 cups syrup.

BUSY-DAY BREAKFAST

Orange Juice
Crisp Bacon
Deluxe Scrambled Eggs
Cinnamon Twists   *Butter*
Coffee   *Milk*

Basic Four Food Value of Menu (see page 5): 1 meat serving, 1½ servings vegetable-fruit, 2 servings bread-cereal, and 1 serving milk.

Special Helps: On hectic days when the family is in a rush to get off to work and school, lure them to the table by giving a new twist to a favorite menu—transform canned biscuits into sweet rolls that are sure to be a hit, especially with the youngsters.
• Make the orange juice quickly in the blender for additional flavor. Fry the bacon while preparing the eggs and tomatoes. Then, cook the eggs and serve breakfast to the family.

DELUXE SCRAMBLED EGGS

For another variation, use large-curd cottage cheese instead of the chopped tomatoes—

    8 eggs
    ⅓ cup milk
    ½ teaspoon salt
      Dash pepper
    2 tablespoons butter or margarine
         • • •
    1 large tomato, chopped
    1 tablespoon snipped parsley

Beat eggs, milk, salt, and pepper together till blended. Melt butter in skillet till hot. Pour in egg mixture. Reduce heat. As mixture begins to set on bottom and sides of skillet, lift and fold with spoon or spatula. Cook till eggs are *almost set;* fold in tomato and parsley. Heat through. Serve immediately. Serves 4.

CINNAMON TWISTS

For a delicious late-night snack, reheat leftover twists and serve with milk or hot chocolate—

    ½ cup sugar
    2 teaspoons ground cinnamon
         • • •
    1 package refrigerated biscuits,
      (10 biscuits)
    ¼ cup butter or margarine, melted
    2 tablespoons chopped walnuts

Combine sugar and cinnamon. Roll a biscuit into a 9-inch rope; bring ends together and seal. Repeat with remaining biscuits. Dip each circle in the melted butter or margarine, then in the cinnamon-sugar mixture. Twist circles into a figure 8; place on greased baking sheet. Sprinkle with nuts. Bake at 450° for about 10 minutes. Serve warm. Makes 4 or 5 servings.

Disguising refrigerated biscuits with a cinnamon-sugar coating and a new shape transforms them into *Cinnamon Twists.*

MIDDAY MEALS

SNOWY DAY LUNCH

Luncheon Special
Buttered Spinach
Carrot Curls
Baked Fruit Dessert   or   *Fresh Fruit*
Milk   *Coffee*

Basic Four Food Value of Menu (see page 5):
1 serving meat, 2½ servings vegetable-fruit,
1 serving bread-cereal, and 1½ servings milk.

Special Helps: To make Carrot Curls, place
peeled carrots on a cutting surface. Using a
vegetable peeler, shave a thin, wide lengthwise
strip of carrot by pushing the peeler away from
you. Roll up the strip and secure with a wood-
en pick. Place in ice-cold water to crisp. Remove the picks from the curls before serving.

BAKED FRUIT DESSERT

  1 16-ounce can peach halves or
     slices, drained
  1 8¾-ounce can pineapple tidbits,
     drained
  1 8¾-ounce can pitted dark sweet
     cherries, drained
  ¼ cup brown sugar
  ½ teaspoon ground cinnamon
  2 tablespoons butter or margarine
    Dairy sour cream

Combine peaches, pineapple, and cherries in
1½-quart casserole. Combine brown sugar and
cinnamon; sprinkle over fruit. Dot with butter.
Bake, covered, at 325° for 15 minutes. Stir
gently just before serving. Serve warm with
dollops of sour cream. Makes 5 or 6 servings.

LUNCHEON SPECIAL

  1 cup yellow cornmeal
  2 cups milk
  1 cup milk
  2 tablespoons salad oil
  1 teaspoon baking powder
  1 teaspoon salt
  3 well-beaten egg yolks
  3 stiffly beaten egg whites

      • • •

  ½ cup chopped celery
  ¼ cup butter or margarine
  ⅓ cup all-purpose flour
  1 13¾-ounce can condensed chicken
     broth
  2 cups cubed, cooked chicken
  2 tablespoons chopped canned
     pimiento
    Salt
    Parsley

Prepare spoon bread by cooking cornmeal and
the 2 cups milk till the consistency of mush.
Remove from heat; stir in the 1 cup milk, salad
oil, baking powder, and 1 teaspoon salt. Add
the beaten egg yolks; fold in beaten egg whites.
Pour spoon bread mixture into a greased 1½-
quart casserole. Bake at 325° for 1 hour.

  Meanwhile, cook celery in butter or margarine till tender but not browned. Blend in
flour. Stir in the condensed chicken broth.
Cook and stir till thickened and bubbly. Add
chicken, chopped canned pimiento, and salt to
taste; heat through. To serve, ladle creamed
chicken mixture over portions of hot spoon
bread. Garnish luncheon plates with parsley,
if desired. Makes 6 servings.

Hot lunch to brighten up a cold day

Combine fluffy spoon bread and a rich, →
creamy chicken mixture for *Luncheon Special,* a superb lunch or supper main dish.

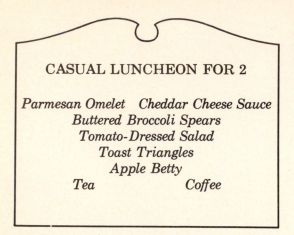

CASUAL LUNCHEON FOR 2

Parmesan Omelet   Cheddar Cheese Sauce
Buttered Broccoli Spears
Tomato-Dressed Salad
Toast Triangles
Apple Betty
Tea   Coffee

Basic Four Food Value of Menu (see page 5): 1 serving meat, 3 servings vegetable-fruit, 1 serving bread-cereal, and 1 serving milk.

Special Helps: Make the salad dressing ahead and chill for best flavor. Return unused portion of the dressing to the refrigerator.

TOMATO-DRESSED SALAD

- ¼ cup catsup
- 1 tablespoon cornstarch
- 1 teaspoon prepared mustard
- 1 cup water
- ¼ cup vinegar
- 2 tablespoons sugar
- 1 tablespoon salad oil
- ½ teaspoon paprika
- ½ teaspoon dried basil leaves, crushed
- ½ teaspoon Worcestershire sauce
- 2 cups torn lettuce
- ¼ cup chopped celery
- 1 tablespoon sliced green onion

In small saucepan blend together catsup, cornstarch, and mustard; add water. Cook over medium heat, stirring constantly, till mixture is thickened and bubbly; cook 1 minute longer. Remove from heat. Stir in vinegar, sugar, oil, paprika, basil, Worcestershire sauce, and dash salt. Chill. Makes 1⅓ cups dressing.

Combine lettuce, celery, and onion in salad bowl. Stir dressing. Add enough dressing to coat leaves lightly; toss. Makes 2 servings.

PARMESAN OMELET

A delightful, light luncheon entrée with double cheese flavor and a gourmet flair—

- 4 egg yolks
- 4 egg whites
- ¼ cup water

· · ·

- ¼ cup grated Parmesan cheese
- 1 tablespoon butter or margarine
  Cheddar Cheese Sauce

Beat egg yolks till thick and lemon-colored; wash and dry beaters. Beat egg whites till frothy; add water and beat till egg whites are stiff but not dry. Fold egg yolk mixture into egg whites. Sprinkle Parmesan cheese over egg mixture; fold in gently. Melt butter or margarine in 10-inch ovenproof skillet; heat till sizzling hot. Pour in the egg mixture. Reduce heat; cook slowly till egg mixture is puffed and golden on the bottom, about 5 minutes. Then, bake at 325° till knife inserted just off-center comes out clean, about 6 to 8 minutes.

Loosen sides of omelet from skillet with spatula. Make a shallow crease across omelet at right angles to skillet handle, just above center. Slip spatula under large half near handle. Tip omelet onto heated serving platter. Spoon Cheddar Cheese Sauce over omelet. Serve immediately. Makes 2 servings.

CHEDDAR CHEESE SAUCE

- 4 teaspoons butter or margarine
- 4 teaspoons all-purpose flour
  Dash salt
- ¾ cup milk

· · ·

- 3 ounces Cheddar cheese, shredded (¾ cup)

In small saucepan melt butter or margarine. Blend in flour and salt. Add milk all at once. Cook, stirring constantly, till mixture is thickened and bubbly. Cook a few minutes more. Remove from heat; add shredded Cheddar cheese. Stir till cheese is melted. Spoon Cheddar Cheese Sauce over Parmesan Omelet.

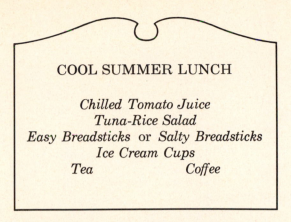

COOL SUMMER LUNCH

Chilled Tomato Juice
Tuna-Rice Salad
Easy Breadsticks or *Salty Breadsticks*
Ice Cream Cups
Tea   *Coffee*

Basic Four Food Value of Menu (see page 5):
1 serving meat, 2 servings vegetable-fruit, 1
serving bread-cereal, and 1½ servings milk.

Special Helps: For a refreshing entrée, prepare Tuna-Rice Salad the night before and
chill. Make either Easy Breadsticks or Salty
Breadsticks for complementary crispness and
flavor. Serve the bread hot from the oven. Or,
for convenience, make the bread earlier and
wrap in plastic bags till lunchtime.
• For an easy dessert, prepare Ice Cream
Cups. Soften chocolate or vanilla ice cream
slightly. Stir in chopped nuts or chopped semisweet chocolate pieces (a blender makes quick
work of chopping). Scoop the ice cream into
colorful paper bake cups and freeze till needed.

EASY BREADSTICKS

  6 slices white bread
  6 tablespoons butter or margarine,
     softened
  1 clove garlic, crushed
  ¼ cup grated Parmesan cheese

Trim crusts from bread, if desired. Blend together butter and crushed garlic; spread on
both sides of bread. Sprinkle both sides of
bread with Parmesan cheese. Cut each slice
into 4 strips. Arrange breadsticks on baking
sheet. Bake at 300° till golden browned on first
side, 10 to 12 minutes. Turn and continue baking on second side till browned, 8 to 10 minutes. Serve breadsticks warm, or cool and wrap
tightly in clear plastic bag. Makes 24 sticks.

TUNA-RICE SALAD

  ¾ cup uncooked long grain rice
  1 10-ounce package frozen peas
  1 9¾-ounce can tuna, drained
  1 8½-ounce can pineapple tidbits,
     drained
  ½ cup chopped celery
     • • •
  ½ cup Thousand Island salad dressing
  ½ cup dairy sour cream
  2 tablespoons finely chopped
     green onion
     • • •
    Lettuce cups

Cook rice following package directions; drain.
Cook peas following package directions; drain.
In bowl combine rice, peas, tuna, pineapple,
and celery. Mix together the Thousand Island
salad dressing, sour cream, and chopped green
onion; pour over rice mixture and toss lightly.
Cover and chill for 12 to 24 hours.
   Before serving, toss tuna mixture lightly.
Spoon into lettuce cups. Makes 6 servings.

SALTY BREADSTICKS

  1⅓ cups sifted all-purpose flour
  2 teaspoons baking powder
  ½ teaspoon salt
  ½ cup cornmeal
  3 tablespoons shortening
     • • •
  ½ cup milk
  1 egg
    Coarse salt

Sift together flour, baking powder, and salt;
stir in cornmeal. Cut in shortening with pastry
blender till mixture resembles coarse crumbs.
Combine milk and egg; add to dry ingredients,
stirring lightly till all is moistened. Turn dough
out on lightly floured surface; knead a few
strokes. Divide dough into 18 pieces. Shape
each piece by rolling under hands into pencil-
like strand about 6 inches long. Place on
greased baking sheet; brush with water and
sprinkle with coarse salt. Bake at 450° for 15
to 18 minutes. Makes 18 breadsticks.

SOUP-SANDWICH LUNCH

Tomato Soup Bonus
Chicken-Fruit Sandwiches
or
Cheesy Ham Sandwiches
Crisp Relishes
Cupcakes
Milk   *Coffee*

Basic Four Food Value of Menu (see page 5): 1 serving meat, 2 servings vegetable-fruit, 2½ servings bread-cereal, and 1 serving milk.

Special Helps: Use your freezer to save time in preparing box lunches by stacking a quantity of sandwiches, such as Chicken-Fruit or Cheesy Ham Sandwiches, and freezing them. Many other fillings freeze well—peanut butter, sliced or ground meats and poultry, Cheddar or cream cheese, fish, and hard-cooked egg yolks. Use these on bread spread with butter or margarine. Wrap sandwiches individually and freeze up to two weeks.

Then, when packing lunches, select the desired sandwich from the freezer. It will thaw in about three hours in the lunch box.

TOMATO SOUP BONUS

  1 10¾-ounce can condensed tomato
      soup
  1 10¾-ounce can condensed
      vegetable soup
1½ soup cans water (2 cups)
 ½ teaspoon lemon juice
 ⅛ teaspoon ground nutmeg

In large saucepan combine tomato soup and vegetable soup; slowly blend in the 1½ cans water. Add lemon juice and nutmeg. Heat to boiling and simmer a few minutes to blend flavors. Rinse vacuum bottles with hot water. Pour in hot soup and close bottles. Makes 4 servings.

CHICKEN-FRUIT SANDWICHES

Good when made with turkey, too—

12 slices white bread
      Butter or margarine, softened
  1 8¾-ounce can crushed pineapple
  2 cups finely chopped, cooked
      chicken *or* turkey
  1 3-ounce package cream cheese,
      softened
  2 tablespoons snipped parsley
 ½ teaspoon salt
      Lettuce leaves

Spread bread slices to the edges with butter. Drain pineapple, reserving syrup. Combine chicken *or* turkey, pineapple, cream cheese, parsley, and salt; blend in 2 to 3 tablespoons reserved pineapple syrup. Spread filling on *6* bread slices, using about ⅓ cup for each; top with remaining bread slices. Wrap each sandwich separately and freeze up to 2 weeks.

As needed, remove sandwiches from freezer. Wrap lettuce separately. Sandwiches will thaw in 2 to 3 hours. Put lettuce on sandwich at lunchtime. Makes 6 sandwiches.

CHEESY HAM SANDWICHES

  8 slices whole wheat or white bread
      Butter or margarine, softened
  1 4½-ounce can deviled ham
  2 ounces process American cheese,
      shredded (½ cup)
  1 tablespoon finely chopped onion
 ½ teaspoon prepared horseradish
      Lettuce leaves
      Tomato slices

Spread bread slices to the edges with butter. Combine deviled ham, cheese, onion, and horseradish. Spread mixture over *4* slices bread; top with remaining bread slices. Wrap sandwiches separately and freeze up to 2 weeks.

As needed, remove sandwiches from freezer. Wrap lettuce and tomatoes separately in clear plastic bags. Sandwiches will thaw in 2 to 3 hours. At lunchtime, place lettuce and tomatoes on sandwich. Makes 4 sandwiches.

HERO LUNCH

Lunch Box Heroes
Lettuce Leaves
Radishes
Corn Chips   or   *Potato Chips*
Peanut Brittle Cookies
Sliced Peaches   or   *Pudding*
Milk   *Coffee*

Basic Four Food Value of Menu (see page 5): 1 serving meat, 2 servings vegetable-fruit, 2½ servings bread-cereal, and 1 serving milk.

Special Helps: Using a small widemouthed vacuum jar to pack desserts adds variety to lunch box menus. For instance, chill canned fruit overnight and then pour into the vacuum jar when packing lunch. If desired, add another ingredient—a sprinkle of coconut or some orange juice—for extra flavor. The fruit will be cool and tasty for lunch.

For a pudding dessert, prepare a favorite pudding as usual and chill thoroughly. Spoon into the small vacuum jar when packing lunch. The vacuum jar will ensure that the dessert is properly stored till lunchtime.

LUNCH BOX HEROES

    ½ cup butter or margarine
    2 teaspoons prepared mustard
    2 teaspoons snipped parsley
       French rolls, split
       Sliced salami, bologna, and
          pickle and pimiento loaf
       Sliced process Swiss cheese
       Lettuce leaves

Cream butter or margarine; stir in mustard and parsley. Spread on split rolls; top with sliced meats and cheese. Place in clear plastic bags or cover with clear plastic wrap. Wrap lettuce separately. At lunchtime, add lettuce.

PEANUT BRITTLE COOKIES

An easy cookie version of peanut brittle candy—

    1 stick piecrust mix
    ¾ cup brown sugar
         • • •
    ¾ cup chopped peanuts
    1 slightly beaten egg
    ½ teaspoon vanilla

Mix piecrust mix according to package directions, but do not roll out. Cut in the brown sugar till mixture resembles coarse crumbs. Add ¼ *cup* of the peanuts, egg, and vanilla; mix well. On a well greased and floured cookie sheet, spread mixture to a 12x12-inch square; press remaining ½ cup peanuts into the dough. Bake at 350° for 15 to 20 minutes. Loosen edges as soon as cookies are removed from oven. Cool on sheet; cut in 2-inch squares. Makes 36.

Wrap lettuce separately when making *Lunch Box Heroes* **so lettuce will stay crisp. Add it to the sandwich just before eating.**

EVENING MEALS

FAMILY GOURMET NIGHT

Chicken Chasseur
Toasted Barley Bake
Crisp Relishes   or   Molded Salad
French Rolls   Butter
Buttersctoch Brownies à la Mode
Coffee   Milk   White Wine

Basic Four Food Value of Menu (see page 5): 1 serving meat, 2 servings vegetable-fruit, 2½ servings bread-cereal, and 1¼ servings milk.

Special Helps: The Chicken Chasseur and Toasted Barley Bake cook in the oven together. So that they will be finished cooking and ready to serve at the same time, prepare the Toasted Barley Bake first and set it aside (do not begin baking just yet). Then, begin cooking the chicken. (If you prefer, substitute ⅔ cup boiling water and 2 chicken bouillon cubes for the ⅔ cup dry white wine.) Set the barley into the oven approximately 5 minutes before you have the Chicken Chasseur ready. This will allow time for the chicken to bake plus time for the final steps of preparing the vegetables and sauce to complete the recipe.
• The rest of the foods in the menu can be made ahead. Prepare the relishes or salad and the brownies earlier in the day or the night before. Clean and slice an assortment of celery sticks, carrot sticks, cauliflowerets, and cucumber slices, and then store these in clear plastic bags. Arrange the vegetables on a tray just before serving time. If a molded salad is preferred, prepare a favorite lime or lemon gelatin with chopped vegetables. Arrange the butterscotch brownies on dessert plates at serving time. Top each serving with a scoop of ice cream and a syrup or liqueur, if desired.

CHICKEN CHASSEUR

¼ cup all-purpose flour
1 teaspoon salt
¼ teaspoon dried oregano leaves, crushed
⅛ teaspoon pepper
8 chicken drumsticks
3 tablespoons butter or margarine
⅔ cup dry white wine
1 tablespoon lemon juice
½ cup chopped onion
1 cup fresh mushrooms, sliced
2 medium tomatoes, peeled and chopped
1 teaspoon sugar

Combine flour, salt, oregano, and pepper. Reserve 1 tablespoon mixture; coat chicken with remaining mixture. In oven-going skillet brown chicken in butter. Combine wine and lemon juice. Pour over chicken. Add onion. Bake, covered, at 350° till tender, about 45 minutes.

Remove chicken to hot platter; keep warm. Add mushrooms, tomatoes, and sugar to mixture in skillet; cook till vegetables are tender, 5 minutes. Blend reserved flour mixture and ¼ cup water; add to sauce. Cook and stir till thick and bubbly. Pour over chicken. Serves 4.

TOASTED BARLEY BAKE

¾ cup quick-cooking barley
¼ cup finely chopped onion
¼ cup butter or margarine
1 chicken bouillon cube
1 tablespoon snipped parsley

In skillet cook barley and onion in butter over low heat, stirring frequently, till onion is tender and barley is golden brown. Stir in 2½ cups boiling water, bouillon cube, and ½ teaspoon salt. Pour into 1-quart casserole dish. Bake, uncovered, at 350° for 1 hour, stirring once or twice. Stir in parsley. Makes 4 to 6 servings.

Serve chicken drumsticks in a grand style. Simmer the
chicken in a wine or a bouillon mixture, and top with a
mushroom-tomato sauce to create *Chicken Chasseur*.

SUNDAY DINNER

Marinated Rump Roast
Mashed Potatoes   Carrot Casserole
Tossed Salad
Hot Rolls   Butter
Slice-O-Lemon Pudding
Coffee   Milk

Basic Four Food Value of Menu (see page 5): 1 serving meat, 3 servings vegetable-fruit, 1 serving bread-cereal, and 1 serving milk.

Special Helps: Organize the preparation of an oven meal so that all the foods will be finished cooking at the same time even though individual baking times are different. In this menu put the roast in first—about 2 hours before dinner for medium doneness or 2½ hours for well-done. (Determine desired doneness by using a meat thermometer inserted into the center of the thickest part of the meat.)

Add the Carrot Casserole ½ hour after the meat or about 1½ hours before serving.

The pudding goes into the oven last. If the oven will accommodate all three foods, add the pudding about 40 minutes before the other foods are done. If the oven is not large enough, put in the pudding when you take out the roast. It will bake while the meat is being carved and dinner eaten. In either case, increase oven temperature to 350° for pudding.

CARROT CASSEROLE

  12 medium carrots, peeled and sliced in ½-inch circles
   1 envelope dry onion soup mix
   2 cups water

Put carrots in 2-quart baking dish; sprinkle with soup mix. Add water. Bake, covered, at 325° till carrots are tender, about 1½ hours. Add water, if needed. Makes 10 servings.

MARINATED RUMP ROAST

  ¾ cup water
  ⅓ cup soy sauce
  2 tablespoons sugar
  1 teaspoon ground ginger
  1 teaspoon dried thyme leaves, crushed
  1 clove garlic, minced
     • • •
  1 3½- to 4-pound boneless rump roast*

Combine first 6 ingredients. Pierce meat several times with a long-tined fork. Place meat in plastic bag; set in deep bowl. Pour marinade in bag and close. Refrigerate overnight. Occasionally turn bag to distribute marinade.

Remove meat from bag; reserve marinade. Put meat on rack in shallow pan. Insert meat thermometer. Roast, uncovered, at 325° about 2 hours for medium doneness, basting with the marinade during last 30 minutes. Strain remaining marinade; heat with 2 tablespoons water. Spoon over meat slices. Serves 8 to 10. *Buy high-quality meat to ensure tenderness.

SLICE-O-LEMON PUDDING

  2 medium lemons
  ¼ cup sliced maraschino cherries (optional)
 1½ cups sugar
  ½ cup butter or margarine
  2 eggs
 1½ cups sifted all-purpose flour
  2 teaspoons baking powder
  ¼ teaspoon salt
  ½ cup milk

Peel lemons and slice *very thin;* arrange lemon slices and cherries in 9x9x2-inch baking pan. Sprinkle with ½ *cup* of the sugar; set aside. Cream together butter or margarine and remaining sugar. Beat in eggs. Sift together flour, baking powder, and salt; add to creamed mixture alternately with milk. Pour 1¼ cups *boiling* water over lemon mixture. Drop batter atop by spoonfuls. Bake at 350° for 40 minutes. Serve warm. Serves 9.

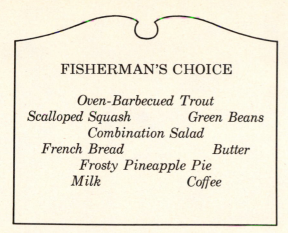

FISHERMAN'S CHOICE

Oven-Barbecued Trout
Scalloped Squash   Green Beans
Combination Salad
French Bread   Butter
Frosty Pineapple Pie
Milk   Coffee

Basic Four Food Value of Menu (see page 5): 1 serving meat, 3 servings vegetable-fruit, 2 servings bread-cereal, and 1½ servings milk.

Special Helps: To carve the whole, cooked fish, use a table knife to make a lengthwise cut about one inch from the upper edge, cutting into the fish just to the backbone. Then, slide knife along top of backbone while lifting top section away from the bone. Repeat with bottom section. Finally, slide the knife under the backbone, lift it up, and discard backbone.

OVEN-BARBECUED TROUT

  ½ cup diced celery
  ½ cup chopped green pepper
  ¼ cup butter or margarine
2½ cups herb-seasoned stuffing
      croutons
  6 pan-dressed trout
      (½ pound each)
      Bottled barbecue sauce

Cook celery and green pepper in butter till tender but not brown; toss with croutons and ½ cup water. Season fish cavities with salt; brush cavities liberally with barbecue sauce. Stuff fish, using about ½ cup stuffing for each. Brush fish with barbecue sauce. Place in shallow baking pan. Cover with foil. Bake at 350° for 35 minutes. Remove foil; brush with additional barbecue sauce. Bake, uncovered, till fish flakes easily when tested with a fork, about 25 minutes. Makes 6 servings.

SCALLOPED SQUASH

  1 pound unpeeled, sliced summer
      squash (3 cups)
  1 medium onion, cut in wedges
  3 tablespoons butter or margarine
  3 tablespoons all-purpose flour
  ½ teaspoon salt
      Dash pepper
1¼ cups milk
  2 ounces process Swiss cheese,
      shredded (½ cup)

Cook squash and onion in boiling, salted water till tender, 8 to 10 minutes; drain. In saucepan melt butter; stir in flour, salt, and pepper. Add milk all at once. Cook and stir till thick and bubbly. Add cheese; stir till melted. Add squash and onion. Pour into 1½-quart casserole. Bake, uncovered, at 350° for 25 to 30 minutes. Makes 6 servings.

FROSTY PINEAPPLE PIE

1½ cups sifted all-purpose flour
  ¼ cup sugar
  ¾ cup butter or margarine
  1 8¾-ounce can crushed pineapple
  1 egg white
  ½ cup sugar
  1 tablespoon lemon juice
  1 cup whipping cream
  1 4-ounce can shredded coconut
      (1⅓ cups)

Blend flour and the ¼ cup sugar. Cut in butter till crumbs are size of small peas. Press *2 cups* of the mixture into greased and floured 9-inch pie plate; crumble remaining mixture into a shallow pan. Bake crumbs at 375° for 10 minutes and bake pie shell for 20 minutes; cool.

   Drain pineapple, reserving ¼ cup of the syrup. Beat egg white till soft peaks form. Gradually add the ½ cup sugar, beating to stiff peaks. Gradually beat in reserved pineapple syrup and lemon juice. Whip cream. Fold in pineapple, coconut, and egg white mixture. Pour into crust. Top with reserved crumbs. Freeze 5 hours. Let stand at room temperature 10 minutes before serving. Serves 6 to 8.

Present *Chicken Cacciatore* as the main attraction in the dinner. Complete the menu with buttered zucchini slices, molded fruit salads, and hot *Parmesan Italian Bread*.

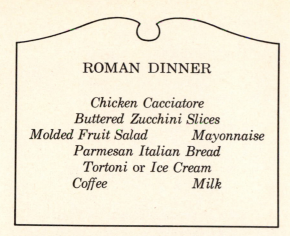

ROMAN DINNER

Chicken Cacciatore
Buttered Zucchini Slices
Molded Fruit Salad   Mayonnaise
Parmesan Italian Bread
Tortoni or *Ice Cream*
Coffee   Milk

Basic Four Food Value of Menu (see page 5):
1 serving meat, 2 servings vegetable-fruit,
1 serving bread-cereal, and 1¼ servings milk.

Special Helps: Chicken Cacciatore is a
versatile recipe. Not only can it be the main
dish for an oven meal, but it also adapts to a
make-ahead meal. To prepare it ahead, follow
the recipe directions through the step where
the tomato and wine mixture is poured over the
chicken. Then, simmer the chicken, covered,
on top of the range for 30 minutes. Turn the
chicken occasionally. Cover and place in the
refrigerator. Store up to 24 hours.

When serving time approaches, cook the
chicken, uncovered, over low heat for about 20
minutes. Turn the chicken once or twice during cooking. Remove to a serving platter and
ladle the tomato sauce over the chicken.
• Canned fruit in a molded salad provides a
wonderful contrast in flavor and texture to the
artfully seasoned Chicken Caccitore in this
menu. For color balance choose an orange- or
lemon-flavored gelatin, and add the family's
favorite fruits, such as diced peaches, mandarin
oranges, or fruit cocktail. Allow 1 cup fruit for
each 3-ounce package of gelatin.

One advantage of canned fruits is that the
juice or syrup in which they are packed can be
used for part of the liquid. Measure the syrup
and add enough water to make 2 cups liquid
for each 3-ounce package of gelatin.

Individual molds are attractive, if you have
them, but don't overlook the possibilities of
custard cups, paper cups, or small drinking
glasses as molds for individual portions.

CHICKEN CACCIATORE

  ¼ cup all-purpose flour
  ½ teaspoon salt
  1 2½- to 3-pound ready-to-cook
       broiler-fryer chicken, cut up
  ¼ cup olive oil *or* salad oil
  ½ cup chopped onion
  ¼ cup chopped celery
  ¼ cup chopped green pepper
  2 cloves garlic, minced
  1 16-ounce can tomatoes, cut up
  1 8-ounce can tomato sauce
  1 3-ounce can sliced mushrooms,
       drained
  ⅓ cup dry white wine
  1 teaspoon salt
  ½ teaspoon dried basil leaves,
       crushed
  ½ teaspoon dried rosemary leaves,
       crushed
     Dash pepper

Combine flour and the ½ teaspoon salt in a
clear plastic bag or paper bag; add a few pieces
of chicken at a time and shake. In an oven-
going skillet brown the chicken in hot oil; remove chicken. In same skillet cook onion, celery, green pepper, and garlic till tender but not
brown. Return chicken to skillet. Combine tomatoes, tomato sauce, mushrooms, wine, the
1 teaspoon salt, basil, rosemary, and pepper.
Pour over chicken. Cover and bake at 350° till
chicken is tender, about 1 hour. Remove the
chicken to warm serving dish. Ladle sauce over
top. Makes 4 servings.

PARMESAN ITALIAN BREAD

  1 unsliced loaf Italian bread
  ½ cup butter or margarine, softened
  ⅓ cup grated Parmesan cheese
  ¼ cup finely snipped chives

Cut Italian bread into 1-inch slices, *cutting to
but not through* bottom crust. Blend together the
butter or margarine, Parmesan cheese, and
snipped chives; spread on one side of each
bread slice. Wrap loaf in foil and heat at 350°
till hot, about 30 minutes. Makes 1 loaf.

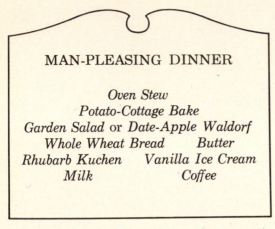

MAN-PLEASING DINNER

Oven Stew
Potato-Cottage Bake
Garden Salad or Date-Apple Waldorf
Whole Wheat Bread   Butter
Rhubarb Kuchen   Vanilla Ice Cream
Milk   Coffee

Basic Four Food Value of Menu (see page 5): 1 serving meat, 3 servings vegetable-fruit, 1½ servings bread-cereal, and 1⅓ servings milk.

Special Helps: Oven Stew, Potato-Cottage Bake, and Rhubarb Kuchen are designed to be baked together. To make sure that the dishes are done at the same time, put the stew in the oven first—about 2½ hours before dinner. Then, prepare the kuchen and put it in to bake 1 hour before dinner. About 35 minutes before serving, add the potatoes.

• If baking only one of these recipes, check the food 20 minutes before the baking time given since it will bake faster if cooked alone.

OVEN STEW

    2 pounds beef stew meat, cut in
        1-inch cubes
    2 tablespoons salad oil
    1 10½-ounce can condensed cream
        of mushroom soup
    1 medium carrot, peeled and
        shredded
    ⅓ cup dry red wine
    1 3-ounce can chopped mushrooms,
        drained
    2 tablespoons dry onion soup mix

In large skillet brown the stew meat in salad oil. Transfer meat to a 2-quart casserole. Combine remaining ingredients; pour over meat. Bake, covered, at 350° for 2½ hours, stirring occasionally. Makes 6 to 8 servings.

RHUBARB KUCHEN

    1 cup sifted all-purpose flour
    3 tablespoons sugar
    1½ teaspoons baking powder
    ¼ teaspoon salt
    6 tablespoons butter or margarine
    1 beaten egg
    2 tablespoons milk
    ½ teaspoon vanilla
    1 3-ounce package strawberry-
        flavored gelatin
    ⅓ cup sugar
    3 tablespoons all-purpose flour
    1¼ pounds rhubarb, sliced (4 cups)
    ⅔ cup sugar
    ⅓ cup sifted all-purpose flour

Combine first 4 ingredients. Cut in *3 tablespoons* butter till mixture resembles coarse crumbs. Combine egg, milk, and vanilla. Add to flour mixture; stir till moistened. Lightly flour hands; pat dough on bottom and 1 inch up the sides of a 9x9x2-inch baking pan.

Combine gelatin, ⅓ cup sugar, and 3 tablespoons flour. Add rhubarb and mix well; pour into crust. Combine ⅔ cup sugar and ⅓ cup flour; cut in 3 tablespoons butter till crumbly. Sprinkle over rhubarb. Bake at 350° till rhubarb is tender and top is browned, 60 to 65 minutes. Cool slightly. Cut in squares; serve with ice cream. Makes 6 to 8 servings.

POTATO-COTTAGE BAKE

    4 medium potatoes, peeled and
        cooked
    1 cup cream-style cottage cheese
    1 egg
    1 teaspoon salt
        Dash pepper
    2 tablespoons snipped parsley
    1 tablespoon butter or margarine

With electric mixer beat potatoes, cottage cheese, egg, salt, and pepper till nearly smooth. Stir in parsley. Turn into well-greased 1-quart casserole. Dot with butter; sprinkle with paprika, if desired. Bake, uncovered, at 350° for 35 minutes. Makes 6 to 8 servings.

Scoop vanilla ice cream atop squares of warm *Rhubarb Kuchen* for a delicious à la mode dessert. Add cups of hot coffee sparked with cinnamon to complete the last course.

GARDEN SALAD

  1 3-ounce package lime-flavored
      gelatin
  1 3-ounce package lemon-flavored
      gelatin
  3 tablespoons lemon juice
1½ teaspoons prepared horseradish
  1 cup finely chopped, unpeeled
      cucumber
  1 cup shredded carrot
 ¼ cup sliced celery
     Lettuce

Dissolve lime and lemon gelatins in 2 cups boiling water. Add 1½ cups cold water, lemon juice, and horseradish. Chill till partially set. Fold in vegetables. Pour into 5½-cup ring mold. Chill till set. Unmold salad onto lettuce. Pass mayonnaise, if desired. Makes 8 servings.

DATE-APPLE WALDORF

  1 orange
  2 cups diced, unpeeled apple
 ½ cup pitted dates, snipped
 ½ cup chopped celery
 ⅓ cup chopped walnuts
 ¼ cup mayonnaise or salad dressing
  1 tablespoon sugar
 ¾ cup frozen whipped dessert
      topping, thawed
     Lettuce cups

Peel orange; section over bowl to catch juices. Halve sections and reserve 1 tablespoon juice. In bowl combine apple, dates, celery, walnuts, and orange. Blend together mayonnaise, sugar, and reserved orange juice. Fold in the thawed dessert topping; combine with date mixture. Serve in lettuce cups. Makes 6 servings.

ROUND STEAK DINNER
(pictured on the cover)

Home-Style Round Steak
Saucy Succotash   Broiled Onion Slices
Fresh Vegetable Platter
Poppy Seed Rolls   Butter
Berry Cheesecake Pie
Coffee   Milk

Basic Four Food Value of Menu (see page 5): 1 serving meat, 3 servings vegetable-fruit, 1½ servings bread-cereal, and 1 serving milk.

Special Helps: Add flavor to a Fresh Vegetable Platter by marinating the vegetables in Italian salad dressing. Just before serving, garnish with snipped parsley.

HOME-STYLE ROUND STEAK

  1½ pounds beef round steak
   2 tablespoons all-purpose flour
   2 tablespoons salad oil
   1 beef bouillon cube, crumbled
   2 tablespoons snipped parsley
   1 teaspoon sugar
   ½ teaspoon dried thyme leaves, crushed
   3 tablespoons all-purpose flour
   ½ teaspoon Kitchen Bouquet

Cut steak in serving-sized pieces; coat both sides with the 2 tablespoons flour. In an oven-going skillet brown the meat in hot oil. Season with salt and pepper. Add 1 cup water, bouillon cube, parsley, sugar, and thyme. Cover and bake at 350° till tender, 1½ to 2 hours. Remove beef to serving platter. Measure pan juices; add enough water to equal 1½ cups. Combine the 3 tablespoons flour and ½ cup cold water. Stir into pan juices; add Kitchen Bouquet. Cook, stirring constantly, till thick and bubbly. Serve gravy over meat. Makes 6 servings.

SAUCY SUCCOTASH

  1 16-ounce can whole kernel corn, drained
  1 10-ounce package frozen cut green beans, cooked and drained
  2 ounces sharp process American cheese, shredded (½ cup)
  ¼ cup chopped celery
  ¼ cup sliced green onion
  ½ cup mayonnaise or salad dressing
  ½ teaspoon Worcestershire sauce
  2 tablespoons butter or margarine
  1 cup soft bread crumbs

Combine corn, beans, cheese, celery, and onion. Combine mayonnaise and Worcestershire sauce; fold into corn mixture. Turn into 1-quart casserole. Melt butter; toss with crumbs. Sprinkle buttered crumbs atop casserole. Bake at 350° for 30 minutes. Makes 6 servings.

BERRY CHEESECAKE PIE

  1 10¾- or 11-ounce package cheesecake mix
  ⅓ cup chopped almonds, toasted
  1 9-inch *baked* pastry shell with high fluted edge, cooled
  1 cup sugar
  2 tablespoons cornstarch
  1 quart fresh strawberries
  1 3-ounce package strawberry-flavored gelatin
  1 tablespoon butter or margarine
  1 tablespoon lemon juice

Prepare cheesecake mix following package directions; stir in nuts. Pour into baked pastry shell; chill 1 hour. In saucepan combine sugar and cornstarch. Mash *1 cup* berries; add water to make 2 cups. Stir into sugar mixture. Cook and stir till thick and bubbly; cook 1 minute more. Remove from heat; strain. Add gelatin, butter, and lemon juice; stir till gelatin dissolves. Chill till partially set.

Spoon *1½ cups* of the gelatin mixture over cheesecake. Slice remaining berries; arrange over pie. Spoon remaining gelatin mixture over berries. Chill till set. Makes 6 to 8 servings.

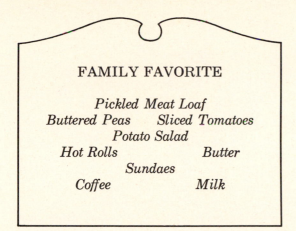

FAMILY FAVORITE

Pickled Meat Loaf
Buttered Peas   *Sliced Tomatoes*
Potato Salad
Hot Rolls   *Butter*
Sundaes
Coffee   *Milk*

Basic Four Food Value of Menu (see page 5): 1 serving meat, 3 servings vegetable-fruit, 1 serving bread, and 1½ servings milk.

Special Helps: When preparing Pickled Meat Loaf, consider making more than you need. Later, use the leftovers in a cold sandwich. Note the leftover section in this book for a picture and a menu that feature another way of using this versatile meat loaf.

POTATO SALAD

        4 cups water
        1 16-ounce package frozen French-
             fried potatoes
    1½ teaspoons salt
        4 hard-cooked eggs, chopped
        ½ cup sliced radish
        ½ cup diced celery
        2 tablespoons sliced green onion
        2 tablespoons snipped parsley
        1 cup mayonnaise or salad dressing
        1 tablespoon vinegar

Pour water into large saucepan; bring to full rolling boil. Carefully drop frozen potatoes into water. Remove from heat immediately; cover and let stand 4 to 5 minutes.

Drain potatoes at once; spread on paper toweling. Cut up any large pieces. Sprinkle potatoes with salt; cool. Blend together remaining ingredients. Add potatoes and toss mixture gently; chill. Garnish with parsley and radish rosettes, if desired. Makes 8 servings.

PICKLED MEAT LOAF

        2 beaten eggs
        ⅓ cup fine dry bread crumbs
        ⅓ cup chili sauce
        1 3-ounce can chopped mushrooms,
             drained
        1 tablespoon prepared horseradish
    1¼ teaspoons salt
        ⅛ teaspoon pepper
        ¼ teaspoon dried thyme leaves,
             crushed
        2 pounds ground beef
             Dill pickles, quartered lengthwise

Combine first 8 ingredients. Add beef; mix well. Pat *half* the mixture into a 9x5x3-inch loaf pan. Top with pickles; cover with rest of mixture. Bake at 350° for 1¼ hours. Serves 8.

Save valuable time when preparing *Potato Salad* by using the convenience product—frozen French-fried potatoes.

SOUTHWESTERN DINNER

Tostado Casserole
Buttered Carrots or Buttered Okra
Guacamole Salad
Tortillas or Corn Chips
Vanilla Ice Cream   Praline Sauce
Milk   Limeade

Basic Four Food Value of Menu (see page 5): 1 serving meat, 3 servings vegetable-fruit, 1½ servings bread-cereal, and 1½ servings milk.

Special Helps: If your family likes spicy foods, treat them to Southwestern-style dishes. The Tostado Casserole is easy to prepare, yet it packs a lot of zippy flavor. For a vegetable, either buttered carrots or okra is a colorful, flavorful addition to the menu. Guacamole Salad, a traditional favorite with Southwestern and Mexican foods, is prepared in this recipe as it's served by many restaurants. (The avocado mixture is also delicous served separately as an appetizer. Just prepare it as usual and use as a guacamole dip with corn chips or tortilla chips.) Praline Sauce over ice cream is the grand finale to this feast.

PRALINE SAUCE

Accent ice cream with rich, praline flavor—

1¼ cups brown sugar
1 6-ounce can evaporated milk
1 tablespoon butter or margarine
½ teaspoon rum flavoring *or* vanilla
⅓ cup chopped pecans

In small saucepan combine brown sugar, evaporated milk, and butter. Cook and stir over low heat till sauce is smooth and syrupy, about 4 to 5 minutes. Stir in rum flavoring *or* vanilla and the pecans. Serve the sauce warm over ice cream. Makes 1⅓ cups sauce.

TOSTADO CASSEROLE

1 pound ground beef
1 15-ounce can tomato sauce
1 envelope taco seasoning mix
2½ cups corn chips
1 15½-ounce can refried beans
2 ounces natural Cheddar cheese, shredded (½ cup)

In skillet brown the ground beef. Add *1½ cups* of the tomato sauce and taco seasoning mix, stirring to mix well. Line bottom of 11¾x7½x 1¾-inch baking dish with *2 cups* of the corn chips; crush remaining corn chips and set aside. Spoon meat mixture over corn chips in baking dish. Combine remaining tomato sauce and beans; spread over cooked meat mixture.

Bake at 375° till mixture is heated through, about 25 minutes. Sprinkle shredded Cheddar cheese and crushed corn chips over the casserole. Continue to bake till the cheese is melted, about 5 minutes more. Makes 6 servings.

GUACAMOLE SALAD

2 ripe avocados, peeled, seeded, and cubed
⅔ cup chopped celery
⅓ cup water
2 tablespoons chopped onion
2 tablespoons lemon juice
1 tablespoon mayonnaise or salad dressing
½ teaspoon salt
¼ teaspoon bottled hot pepper sauce
⅛ teaspoon garlic salt
3 cups shredded lettuce
3 tomatoes, cut in wedges

Place avocados, celery, water, onion, lemon juice, mayonnaise, salt, hot pepper sauce, and garlic salt in blender container. Blend till mixture is smooth. Stop blender occasionally to push food into the blades, if necessary.

Arrange shredded lettuce on 6 chilled salad plates. Place tomato wedges on lettuce and top with guacamole mixture. If desired, sprinkle additional bottled hot pepper sauce over the guacamole. Makes 6 servings.

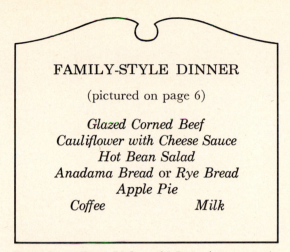

FAMILY-STYLE DINNER

(pictured on page 6)

Glazed Corned Beef
Cauliflower with Cheese Sauce
Hot Bean Salad
Anadama Bread or Rye Bread
Apple Pie
Coffee   *Milk*

Basic Four Food Value of Menu (see page 5): 1 serving meat, 2½ servings vegetable-fruit, 1½ servings bread-cereal, and 1½ servings milk.

Special Helps: If your family loves corned beef but you rarely serve it because of the lengthy cooking time, try a make-ahead meal. Cook the corned beef ahead, either the evening before or earlier in the day when you have extra time, and refrigerate the meat till dinner. Round out the menu with other make-ahead or jiffy dishes and see how quickly you can serve a delicious corned beef dinner after returning from a day at work or a meeting. Cook Glazed Corned Beef by simmering or, if the corned beef is pretendered, by oven-roasting. The package directions will give complete details for the cooking procedures. When the meat is done, drain, wrap, and place it in the refrigerator. At serving time, score the top of the corned beef and sprinkle with brown sugar. Heat in a 350° oven just long enough to glaze the top. Give the main dish an additional touch by garnishing the platter. Arrange sprigs of watercress or parsley, cherry tomatoes, and spiced peaches around the corned beef for a main dish that's as attractive as it is tasty.

To complement the corned beef, also prepare Hot Bean Salad ahead. The marinade seasons the Italian green beans and onions while they are being chilled. Anadama Bread completes the make-ahead list. This distinctive, New England bread is a treat for homemade bread lovers. However, if time does not allow, substitute a loaf of rye bread to complete the menu.

ANADAMA BREAD

  2 packages active dry yeast
5½ to 5¾ cups sifted all-purpose
     flour
  ½ cup cornmeal
  2 cups boiling water
  ½ cup dark molasses
  ⅓ cup shortening
  1 tablespoon salt
  2 eggs

In large bowl combine yeast and *3 cups* flour. Gradually stir cornmeal into boiling water. Add molasses, shortening, and salt. Cool to lukewarm. Add to mixture in bowl; add eggs. Beat at low speed with electric mixer for ½ minute, scraping bowl constantly. Beat 3 minutes at high speed. By hand, stir in enough of the remaining flour to make a soft dough. Turn out on lightly floured surface. Knead till smooth, 7 to 10 minutes. Place in greased bowl; turn once to grease surface. Cover. Let rise in warm place till double, 1½ hours. Punch down. Divide dough in half. Let rest, covered, 10 minutes. Shape in loaves; place in 2 greased 9x5x3-inch loaf pans. Cover; let rise till double, 45 to 60 minutes. Brush with additional melted shortening; bake at 375° for 40 minutes. Cover with foil after 20 minutes if tops are getting too brown.

HOT BEAN SALAD

  ½ cup salad oil
  2 tablespoons vinegar
  ¾ teaspoon sugar
  ¾ teaspoon salt
  ½ teaspoon celery seed
  ¼ teaspoon caraway seed
  ¼ teaspoon paprika
  2 10-ounce packages frozen Italian
     green beans, cooked and drained
  1 small onion, sliced and separated
     into rings

In screw-top jar combine first 7 ingredients; cover and shake well. Pour over beans and onions. Chill 4 to 24 hours. Heat bean mixture till hot through; drain. Makes 6 to 8 servings.

Ladle *Hearty Hodgepodge,* a mixture of beef, ham, sausage, potatoes, and garbanzo beans, into bowls, and pass slices of toasted *Sourdough Bread* for a man-pleasing dinner.

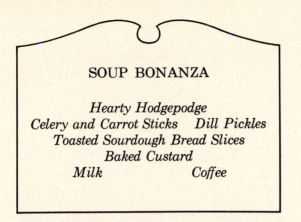

SOUP BONANZA

Hearty Hodgepodge
Celery and Carrot Sticks   Dill Pickles
Toasted Sourdough Bread Slices
Baked Custard
Milk   Coffee

Basic Four Food Value of Menu (see page 5): 1 serving meat, 2 servings vegetable-fruit, 1 serving bread-cereal, and 1⅓ servings milk.

Special Helps: Either make this menu ahead or serve it immediately after preparing. If making it ahead, shorten the initial cooking time for the soup slightly, refrigerate up to 24 hours, skim off fat, and reheat. The flavors will season and improve during storage.

HEARTY HODGEPODGE

    6 slices bacon
    1 medium onion, thinly sliced
    1 pound beef shank
    ¾ pound ham hock
    6 cups water
    2 teaspoons salt
    2 15-ounce cans garbanzo beans
    3 cups diced, peeled potatoes
    1 clove garlic, minced
    1 4-ounce link Polish sausage,
        thinly sliced

In Dutch oven cook bacon till crisp; drain, reserving 2 tablespoons drippings. Crumble bacon and set aside. Cook onions in reserved drippings till tender but not brown. Add beef shank, ham hock, water, and salt. Cover and simmer 1½ hours. Remove meat from shank and ham hock; dice. Skim fat from broth. Return diced meat to soup; add undrained beans, potatoes, and garlic. Simmer, covered, 30 minutes more. Add sausage and bacon. Simmer, covered, 15 minutes longer. Serves 8 to 10.

SOURDOUGH BREAD

Make starter this week for next week's baking—

    1 package active dry yeast
    2½ cups warm water
    2 cups sifted all-purpose flour
    1 tablespoon sugar
        •   •   •
    1 package active dry yeast
    1½ cups warm water
    2 teaspoons salt
    2 teaspoons sugar
    5¼ to 5½ cups sifted all-purpose flour
    ½ teaspoon soda
        •   •   •
    ¾ cup water
    ¾ cup sifted all-purpose flour
    1 teaspoon sugar

To prepare sourdough starter: Dissolve 1 **package** yeast in ½ *cup* of the warm water. Stir in remaining warm water, 2 cups flour, and 1 tablespoon sugar. Beat till smooth. Let stand, covered with cheesecloth, at room temperature for 5 to 10 days. (Time required to ferment depends on room temperature. Starter should have a "yeasty," not sour, smell.) Stir 2 or 3 times a day. Cover; refrigerate till ready to use.

To prepare bread: In a large bowl soften 1 package yeast in 1½ cups warm water. Blend in *1 cup* of the sourdough starter, 2 teaspoons salt, and 2 teaspoons sugar. Add *2½ cups* of the flour. Beat 3 to 4 minutes with electric mixer. Cover; let rise till double, about 1½ hours. Combine soda and *2½ cups* of the flour; stir into dough. Add enough remaining flour for a stiff dough. Turn out onto lightly floured surface; knead 5 to 7 minutes. Divide dough in half; cover and let rest 10 minutes. Shape in 2 round or oval loaves. Place on lightly greased baking sheets. Make diagonal gashes across top with sharp knife. Let rise till double, about 1 to 1½ hours. Bake at 400° for 35 to 40 minutes. Brush with butter or margarine. To serve, slice bread and toast, if desired.

To keep starter: To leftover starter add ¾ cup water, ¾ cup flour, and 1 teaspoon sugar. Let stand till bubbly and well fermented—at least 1 day. Store in refrigerator. If not used within 10 days, add 1 teaspoon sugar.

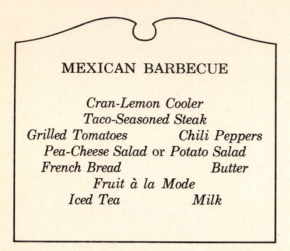

MEXICAN BARBECUE

Cran-Lemon Cooler
Taco-Seasoned Steak
Grilled Tomatoes   Chili Peppers
Pea-Cheese Salad or Potato Salad
French Bread   Butter
Fruit à la Mode
Iced Tea   Milk

Basic Four Food Value of Menu (see page 5): 1½ servings meat, 3½ servings vegetable-fruit, 1 serving bread-cereal, and 1½ servings milk.

Special Helps: The cook is not the only one who benefits from make-ahead cooking techniques. Many foods taste better when made ahead. For instance, the Cran-Lemon Cooler has time to chill thoroughly, so it's even more refreshing when served. The Taco-Seasoned Steak absorbs the zippy flavors of the marinade, whether made with the sherry or tequila. The Pea-Cheese Salad or the potato salad is tastier if prepared ahead because the flavors blend and improve. Likewise, the Fruit à la Mode not only chills but the spicy flavor mingles with the fruits when made ahead.

CRAN-LEMON COOLER

Serve as an appetizer or a beverage on hot days—

>   2 cups water
>   ½ cup sugar
>   2 cups cranberry juice cocktail
>   ½ cup lemon juice
>   Ice cubes (optional)
>   Lemon slices

Combine water and sugar. Stir to dissolve. Add cranberry juice cocktail and lemon juice. Chill thoroughly. At serving time, pour over ice cubes, if desired. Garnish glasses with lemon slices. Makes 6 servings.

TACO-SEASONED STEAK

Marinate round steak in tequila and taco seasoning mix for a unique barbecue entrée—

>   1 envelope taco seasoning mix
>   1 cup water
>   ¼ cup tequila *or* dry sherry
>   1 3-pound round steak, cut 1½
>   to 2 inches thick

Combine taco seasoning mix, water, and tequila *or* sherry. Trim excess fat from round steak; slash the fat edge at 1-inch intervals. Place meat in a large clear plastic bag in a deep bowl. Pour taco marinade into the bag. Seal and marinate several hours or overnight in the refrigerator, turning once.

Drain steak, reserving marinade. Grill steak over *medium* coals 3 inches from heat for a total of 30 to 35 minutes for rare doneness, turning steak frequently and basting with reserved marinade each time. Garnish with parsley and chili peppers, if desired. Slice steak across grain to serve. Makes 6 servings.

FRUIT À LA MODE

>   1 20-ounce can frozen, pitted, tart
>   red cherries, thawed
>   1 10-ounce package frozen peach
>   slices, thawed
>   • • •
>   ¼ cup sugar
>   4 inches stick cinnamon
>   ½ teaspoon whole cloves
>   Few drops red food coloring
>   1 pint vanilla ice cream

Drain thawed fruits, reserving syrups. In saucepan combine reserved syrups, sugar, stick cinnamon, whole cloves, and food coloring. Bring mixture to boiling; reduce heat. Simmer, uncovered, for 10 minutes; strain. Place cherries and peach slices in medium-sized bowl; pour syrup mixture over fruit. Cover and chill for 6 to 24 hours; stir fruit occasionally.

Spoon fruit mixture into individual dessert dishes; top each serving with a scoop of vanilla ice cream. Makes 6 servings.

Experiment with various cuts of meat for barbecuing. Round steak is used in *Taco-Seasoned Steak*, for instance, to make a tasty, economical entrée for a family meal.

GRILLED TOMATOES

Corn chip topping adds crunch and flavor—

   3 large, firm tomatoes
     Salt
     Pepper
     . . .
  ¼ cup crushed corn chips
   2 tablespoons butter or margarine, melted
   2 tablespoons snipped parsley
  ¼ teaspoon garlic salt

Slice tomatoes in half; sprinkle liberally with salt and pepper. Combine corn chips, butter, parsley, and garlic salt. Sprinkle over tomato halves. Place in an 11x7x1½-inch baking pan. Cook, uncovered, on the edge of the grill till heated through, about 15 to 20 minutes. Serve immediately. Makes 6 servings.

PEA-CHEESE SALAD

   1 16-ounce package frozen peas, cooked and drained
   4 ounces natural Cheddar cheese, cubed (1 cup)
   2 hard-cooked eggs, chopped
  ¼ cup finely chopped celery
   2 tablespoons finely chopped onion
   2 tablespoons chopped canned pimiento
  ⅓ cup mayonnaise or salad dressing
  ¼ teaspoon salt
  ¼ teaspoon bottled hot pepper sauce

In large bowl combine peas, cheese cubes, hard-cooked eggs, celery, onion, and chopped pimiento. Combine mayonnaise or salad dressing, salt, and hot pepper sauce; add to salad. Toss. Cover and refrigerate several hours or overnight. Makes 6 servings.

WEEKEND COOKOUT

Hot Barbecue Ribs
Corn on the Cob
Horseradish Butter   Herbed Butter
Vegetable-Dill Combo
or
Tossed Green Salad
Bread   Butter
Marshmallow Ice Cream
Lemonade   Milk

Basic Four Food Value of Menu (see page 5): 1 serving meat, 2 servings vegetable-fruit, 1 serving bread-cereal, and 1½ servings milk.

Special Helps: Corn on the cob is a summertime favorite that goes well with Hot Barbecue Ribs. Roast the corn alongside the ribs on the grill to make use of the charcoal fire, or cook the corn in the oven if there is not room for ribs and corn on the grill.

If you are planning to cook corn on the cob on the grill, first remove the husks from fresh ears of corn. Then, remove the silks with a stiff brush. Place each ear of corn on a piece of foil. Spread the corn liberally with butter or margarine, and season with salt and pepper.

Next, wrap the foil around the ear of corn (do not seal the seam—this causes the corn to steam rather than roast) and twist or fold the ends. Place the corn on the grill along with the meat and cook till tender, about 12 to 25 minutes. Turn the corn often, being careful not to puncture the foil wrap with a barbecue tool. Pass Horseradish Butter and Herbed Butter or extra butter with additional salt and pepper for each person to season his or her ear of corn according to personal preference.

On the other hand, if the corn is to be cooked in the oven rather than on the grill, prepare the corn the same as for grilling, but bake the foil-wrapped ears of corn at 450° till tender—generally about 25 minutes. During cooking, turn the ears of corn several times.

HOT BARBECUE RIBS

  6 pounds country-style pork ribs
¼ cup light molasses
¼ cup prepared mustard
    • • •
¼ cup lemon juice
  1 tablespoon Worcestershire sauce
½ teaspoon bottled hot pepper sauce
¼ teaspoon salt
   Lemon slices

Simmer ribs, covered, in salted water to cover till tender, 45 to 60 minutes; drain. Meanwhile, in small saucepan gradually blend molasses into mustard; stir in lemon juice, Worcestershire sauce, hot pepper sauce, and salt. Heat to boiling. Grill ribs over *slow* to *medium* coals for 10 to 15 minutes on each side, brushing often with barbecue sauce. Garnish ribs with lemon slices. Makes 6 to 8 servings.

VEGETABLE-DILL COMBO

Use an ice bucket for an attractive serving container that also keeps the food cool—

¼ cup creamy French salad dressing
¼ cup mayonnaise or salad dressing
  2 tablespoons chili sauce
  2 teaspoons lemon juice
1¼ teaspoon salt
  1 teaspoon dried dillweed
⅛ teaspoon pepper
1½ cups diced carrots, cooked and
     drained
½ small head cauliflower, sliced,
     cooked, and drained (1½ cups)
  1 9-ounce package frozen peas,
     cooked and drained
  1 9-ounce package frozen Italian
     green beans, cooked and drained
½ cup chopped celery
¼ cup chopped onion

Blend together the French dressing, mayonnaise, chili sauce, lemon juice, salt, dillweed, and pepper. Chill several hours or overnight. Place vegetables in large bowl. Add dressing; toss to coat. Makes 8 servings.

Give a zippy flavor to *Hot Barbecue Ribs* by basting ribs during cooking with a mixture of molasses, mustard, lemon juice, Worcestershire sauce, and hot pepper sauce.

HORSERADISH BUTTER

  ½ cup butter or margarine, softened
  1 tablespoon prepared mustard
  2 teaspoons prepared horseradish
  ½ teaspoon salt
    Dash freshly ground pepper

Combine butter, mustard, horseradish, salt, and pepper. Cream till light and fluffy. Garnish with snipped parsley, if desired. Serve with corn on the cob. Makes about ½ cup.

HERBED BUTTER

Cream ½ cup butter or margarine, softened, till fluffy. Stir in 1 teaspoon dried rosemary leaves, crushed, and ½ teaspoon dried marjoram leaves, crushed. Serve herbed butter with corn on the cob. Makes about ½ cup.

MARSHMALLOW ICE CREAM

A treat of fluffy, soft-serve ice cream that you make at home—

  2 eggs
  ¾ cup sugar
  1 7-ounce jar marshmallow creme
  3 cups milk
  1 cup whipping cream
 1½ teaspoons vanilla

In large mixer bowl beat eggs with electric mixer or rotary beater till light; gradually beat in sugar till thick. Blend in marshmallow creme. Then, blend in the milk, whipping cream, and vanilla. Turn milk mixture into a 1-gallon ice cream freezer container; freeze according to manufacturer's directions. Serve ice cream with a fresh fruit or sundae topping, if desired. Makes 2 quarts ice cream.

Dip fresh fruit into orange juice to retard browning so that both *Fresh Fruit Salad* and *Berry Dressing* can be made ahead.

SUNDAY DIET DINNER

Lime-Basted Chicken
Boiled Potatoes
Seasoned Green Beans
Fresh Fruit Salad   Berry Dressing
Pound Cake
Tea   Skim Milk

Basic Four Food Value of Menu (see page 5): 1 serving meat, 3 servings vegetable-fruit, 1 serving bread-cereal, and 1 serving milk.

Special Helps: You can prepare tasty vegetables without adding extra calories. For example, to prepare Seasoned Green Beans, cook fresh green beans in little or no water over low to medium heat till tender. Then, add lemon juice or an herb to flavor the vegetable instead of adding butter or margarine. Choose basil, dill, marjoram, nutmeg, oregano, savory, or thyme to accent the green beans. Begin with ¼ teaspoon dried herb leaves, crushed, or ¾ teaspoon snipped fresh herb for each 4 servings. Taste, and add more herb till the flavor suits your personal preference.

FRESH FRUIT SALAD

    2 medium oranges, peeled
    1 medium banana, peeled
    1 medium pear
    1 medium peach, peeled
           . . .
      Romaine leaves
    1 cup fresh raspberries

Section oranges, reserving juice in shallow bowl. Slice banana, pear, and peach into reserved orange juice; turn fruit to coat all sides with juice. Chill. Arrange romaine leaves in salad bowl. Top with chilled fruit and raspberries. Serve with Berry Dressing. Makes 6 servings. (77 calories / serving.)

LIME-BASTED CHICKEN

Accent baked chicken with lime juice and peel for an intriguing low-calorie main dish—

    2 tablespoons butter or margarine, melted
    2 tablespoons all-purpose flour
    • • •
    ¼ teaspoon grated lime peel
    2 tablespoons lime juice
    ½ teaspoon salt
      Few drops bottled hot pepper sauce
    • • •
    3 large chicken breasts, halved and skinned

Cream melted butter or margarine and flour together; stir in lime peel, lime juice, salt, and bottled hot pepper sauce. Spread over skinned chicken breasts. Place chicken breasts in an 11¾x7½x1¾-inch baking dish. Bake at 350° till tender, about 50 to 60 minutes. Makes 6 servings. (147 calories / serving.)

BERRY DRESSING

Combine strawberries and low-calorie blackberry jelly to make a dressing for Fresh Fruit Salad—

    ½ cup fresh strawberries
    2 tablespoons sugar
    ¼ cup low-calorie blackberry jelly
    ¼ cup water
    • • •
    1 tablespoon water
    2 teaspoons cornstarch
    1 tablespoon lemon juice

In small saucepan combine fresh strawberries, sugar, low-calorie blackberry jelly, and the ¼ cup water. Bring mixture to boiling; reduce heat and simmer, uncovered, for 15 minutes. Blend the 1 tablespoon water into the cornstarch; stir into strawberry mixture. Cook and stir till mixture is thickened and bubbly. Cook and stir 1 minute longer. Stir in lemon juice. Sieve mixture; discard pulp and seeds. Chill.
  Serve dressing with Fresh Fruit Salad. Makes about ⅔ cup. (21 calories / tablespoon.)

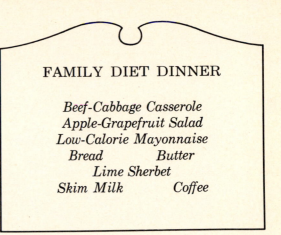

FAMILY DIET DINNER

Beef-Cabbage Casserole
Apple-Grapefruit Salad
Low-Calorie Mayonnaise
Bread   Butter
Lime Sherbet
Skim Milk   Coffee

Basic Four Food Value of Menu (see page 5): 1 serving meat, 3 servings vegetable-fruit, 1 serving bread-cereal, and 1½ servings milk.

Special Helps: To prepare Apple-Grapefruit Salad, arrange wedges of unpeeled apple and grapefruit sections on individual salad plates. Drizzle each with one tablespoon low-calorie French or mayonnaise-type dressing.

BEEF-CABBAGE CASSEROLE

    1½ pounds lean ground beef
    ½ cup chopped onion
    ½ cup chopped green pepper
    1 16-ounce can tomatoes, cut up
    1 teaspoon salt
    1 teaspoon garlic salt
    1 head cabbage (about 2 pounds)
    3 ounces process Swiss cheese, shredded (¾ cup)

In skillet cook beef, onion, and green pepper till meat is browned; drain off fat. Stir in tomatoes, salt, and garlic salt. Simmer, uncovered, 15 minutes, stirring frequently.
  Cut cabbage into 6 wedges. Cook in small amount of boiling, salted water, covered, for 10 to 12 minutes; drain well. Arrange cabbage in 9x9x2-inch baking dish. Pour meat mixture evenly over and around cabbage. Bake, uncovered, at 350° till hot through, 20 to 25 minutes. Sprinkle Swiss cheese over meat mixture. Bake, uncovered, 2 to 3 minutes longer. Makes 6 servings. (291 calories / serving.)

ORIENTAL EVENING

Shrimp-Vegetable Dinner
Red Sauce
Hot Mustard Sauce or *Mustard Sauce*
Hot Rice
Chilled Mandarin Orange Sections
Fortune Cookies
Hot Broth   Green Tea   Milk

Basic Four Food Value of Menu (see page 5): 1 serving meat, 3 servings vegetable-fruit, 1½ servings bread-cereal, and 1 serving milk.

Special Helps: The calorie count of this menu is low because the foods are cooked in boiling broth as is the traditional Chinese Hot Pot. (This avoids the extra calories usually added when foods are fried in fats.) The broth is poured into cups after cooking and is served with dinner for a tasty, low-calorie beverage.

RED SAUCE

    ¼ cup catsup
    1 teaspoon vinegar
    ¼ teaspoon prepared horseradish
       Dash bottled hot pepper sauce

Blend together all ingredients. Chill. Serve with Shrimp-Vegetable Dinner. Makes ¼ cup sauce. (18 calories / tablespoon.)

HOT MUSTARD SAUCE

    ¼ cup boiling water
    ¼ cup dry mustard
    ½ teaspoon salt
    1 tablespoon salad oil

Stir boiling water into dry mustard; add salt and salad oil. Blend thoroughly. Makes about ⅓ cup sauce. (25 calories / tablespoon.)

SHRIMP-VEGETABLE DINNER

    3 13¾-ounce cans chicken broth
       (not condensed)
    ¼ teaspoon ground ginger
           •   •   •
    1 pound fresh or frozen, shelled
       shrimp, thawed
    3 cups small, fresh spinach leaves,
       with stems removed
 1½ cups fresh mushrooms, halved
    1 cup celery, cut into 1-inch pieces
    1 tomato, cut in wedges
    ½ cup green onion, cut into 1-inch
       pieces

Combine chicken broth and ginger in an electric skillet. Bring to a gentle boil. Cook a small amount of the shrimp, spinach, mushrooms, celery, tomato, and green onion in the boiling broth till done, about 3 to 5 minutes. Lift food from broth with slotted spoon; drain. Keep food warm while cooking remaining shrimp and vegetables. Repeat till all is cooked.

When cooking is completed, pour broth into cups to serve as a beverage with dinner. Makes 4 servings. (201 calories / serving.)

MUSTARD SAUCE

    1 tablespoon butter or margarine
    1 tablespoon all-purpose flour
    ⅛ teaspoon salt
       Dash white pepper
    ½ cup skim milk
    1 tablespoon prepared mustard

Melt butter or margarine in saucepan over low heat. Blend in flour, salt, and pepper. Add milk all at once. Cook and stir till thickened and bubbly. Remove from heat; blend in mustard. Makes ½ cup sauce. (24 calories / tablespoon.)

Diet in a foreign atmosphere

Add interest to low-calorie menus by going →
oriental. *Shrimp-Vegetable Dinner*, rice,
and mandarin oranges set the mood.

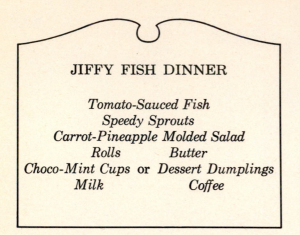

JIFFY FISH DINNER

Tomato-Sauced Fish
Speedy Sprouts
Carrot-Pineapple Molded Salad
Rolls   Butter
Choco-Mint Cups or *Dessert Dumplings*
Milk   Coffee

Basic Four Food Value of Menu (see page 5): 1 serving meat, 2 servings vegetable-fruit, 2 servings bread-cereal, and 1½ servings milk.

Special Helps: The most satisfactory way to thaw fish is to place it in the refrigerator. It takes about 24 hours to thaw a one-pound package. Another method of thawing is to place the wrapped package under cold, running water. This takes only one or two hours.

TOMATO-SAUCED FISH

An herb, lemon, and tomato mixture accents the delicate flavor of haddock or other fish—

  2 pounds fresh or frozen haddock
      fillets or other fish fillets

     • • •

     Salt
  1 3-ounce can sliced mushrooms,
      drained
  1 8-ounce can tomato sauce
  1 tablespoon lemon juice
  ¼ teaspoon dried thyme leaves,
      crushed

Thaw frozen fish fillets; arrange fillets in single layer in well-greased 11½x7½x2-inch baking dish. Sprinkle with salt. Top with drained mushrooms. Blend together the tomato sauce, lemon juice, and thyme; pour over fish. Bake, covered, at 350° till fish flakes easily when tested with a fork, 30 to 35 minutes. If desired, sprinkle with Parmesan cheese. Serves 6.

SPEEDY SPROUTS

  2 10-ounce packages frozen Brussels
      sprouts
  ½ cup mayonnaise or salad dressing
  2 tablespoons grated Parmesan
      cheese
  ¼ teaspoon celery seed
  ¼ teaspoon curry powder

In large saucepan cook Brussels sprouts according to package directions; drain. Blend together the mayonnaise or salad dressing, Parmesan cheese, celery seed, and curry powder. Toss with hot Brussels sprouts. Makes 6 to 8 servings.

CHOCO-MINT CUPS

  1 6-ounce package *regular*
      chocolate pudding mix
  ¾ cup miniature marshmallows
  ¾ teaspoon peppermint extract

Prepare and cook chocolate pudding mix according to package directions; remove from heat. Add miniature marshmallows and peppermint extract, stirring just till marshmallows begin to melt. Spoon pudding into 6 dessert dishes. Serve warm or cold. Makes 6 servings.

DESSERT DUMPLINGS

  ¾ cup brown sugar
  ¾ cup water
  ¼ cup light corn syrup
  2 tablespoons butter or margarine
  1 teaspoon vanilla
  1 package refrigerated biscuits
      (6 biscuits)
     Dairy sour cream

In medium saucepan combine brown sugar, water, corn syrup, butter or margarine, and vanilla. Cook and stir till bubbly; place biscuits on top of mixture. Simmer, uncovered, for 10 minutes. Cover, and continue to simmer 10 minutes. Spoon dumplings into dessert dishes; ladle sauce over top. Serve warm with a dollop of dairy sour cream. Makes 6 servings.

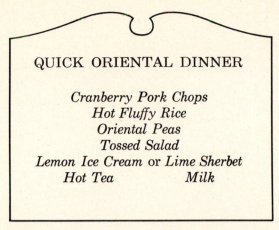

QUICK ORIENTAL DINNER

Cranberry Pork Chops
Hot Fluffy Rice
Oriental Peas
Tossed Salad
Lemon Ice Cream or *Lime Sherbet*
Hot Tea   *Milk*

Basic Four Food Value of Menu (see page 5): 1 serving meat, 2½ servings vegetable-fruit, 1 serving bread-cereal, and 1¼ servings milk.

Special Helps: Cook rice perfectly every time by testing for doneness. Pinch a grain between thumb and forefinger. It is done if there is no hard core remaining in the rice.

CRANBERRY PORK CHOPS

  4 pork chops, cut ¾ inch thick
    Salt and pepper
  1 8½-ounce can pineapple slices
  ½ cup boiling water
  1 chicken bouillon cube
  ½ cup whole cranberry sauce
  2 tablespoons brown sugar
  2 tablespoons vinegar
  1 green pepper, cut in 1-inch strips
  2 tablespoons cornstarch

Trim fat from chops. In skillet cook trimmings till 1 tablespoon fat accumulates; discard trimmings. Brown the chops. Season with salt and pepper. Drain pineapple, reserving syrup. Combine boiling water, bouillon cube, cranberry sauce, brown sugar, vinegar, and reserved syrup; add to chops. Cover and simmer 40 minutes. Add pineapple and green pepper; cover and cook 10 minutes more. Remove chops and pineapple. Combine cornstarch and 2 tablespoons cold water; stir into cranberry mixture. Cook and stir till thick and bubbly. Pour over chops. Serves 4.

ORIENTAL PEAS

Crisp, brightly colored Chinese pea pods are accented by crunchy water chestnuts—

  ¼ cup chopped green onion
  1 tablespoon butter or margarine
  1 7-ounce package frozen Chinese
     pea pods, thawed
  1 5-ounce can water chestnuts,
     drained and sliced (⅔ cup)

      • • •

  ¼ cup hot water
  2 teaspoons soy sauce
  ½ teaspoon salt

Cook onion in butter till tender but not brown. Add pea pods and water chestnuts. Toss and cook over high heat for 1 minute. Add water, soy sauce, and salt; cover and cook over medium heat for 3 minutes. Makes 4 servings.

Treat sweet-and-sour fans in the family to a unique main dish, *Cranberry Pork Chops,* **which is made with cranberry sauce.**

AUTUMNFEST

Cups of Hot Soup
Sausage Casserole
Coleslaw
Bread   Butter
Applesauced Gingerbread
Milk   Coffee

Basic Four Food Value of Menu (see page 5): 1 serving meat, 2 servings vegetable-fruit, 1½ servings bread-cereal, and 1 serving milk.

Special Helps: Select a clear or cream soup to serve in cups or soup bowls as an appetizer before a family dinner. Try serving the soup in a different place, such as in the living room or on the patio. You'll find that an appetizer course of this nature has many advantages. Not only is it easy to prepare, but it also lends a special mood to the dinner—makes the family feel and act more like guests. In addition, the appetizer can be served 10 to 15 minutes before the foods in the main course are done, so a hungry family can be fed sooner.

COLESLAW

Celery salt is included in the salad dressing to accent the flavor of the cabbage—

3   cups shredded cabbage
¼   cup chopped green pepper
2   tablespoons chopped onion
3   tablespoons salad oil
3   tablespoons vinegar
1   teaspoon celery salt
1   teaspoon sugar

Toss shredded cabbage, chopped green pepper, and onion together. In screw-top jar combine salad oil, vinegar, celery salt, and sugar; shake till well blended. Pour dressing over cabbage mixture; toss lightly. Makes 4 to 6 servings.

SAUSAGE CASSEROLE

1   20-ounce can pineapple chunks
     (juice pack)
1   18-ounce can sweet potatoes,
     sliced 1 inch thick
1   12-ounce package smoked link
     sausages, slashed at 1-inch
     intervals
3   tablespoons brown sugar
2   tablespoons cornstarch
¼   teaspoon salt
1   tablespoon butter or margarine

Drain pineapple, reserving juice. Add water to juice if necessary to equal 1¼ cups. Arrange pineapple chunks, sweet potatoes, and sausages in 10x6x1¾-inch baking dish. In small saucepan combine brown sugar, cornstarch, and salt. Gradually blend in reserved pineapple juice mixture. Cook and stir till thickened and bubbly; cook and stir 1 minute more. Remove from heat; stir in butter or margarine. Pour over sausage mixture in baking dish. Cover and bake at 350° till heated through, 35 to 40 minutes. Makes 4 to 6 servings.

APPLESAUCED GINGERBREAD

Use either applesauce or cubes of jellied cranberry sauce in the topping—

1   2-ounce envelope dessert topping
     mix
½   cup chunk-style applesauce *or*
     ½ cup jellied cranberry sauce,
     cut into ¼-inch cubes
1   package gingerbread mix
     Chopped walnuts

Prepare dessert topping mix using package directions; fold in applesauce *or* cranberry cubes. (When using applesauce, tint with a few drops of yellow food coloring, if desired.) Chill till ready to serve.

Prepare gingerbread mix according to package directions; bake in a 9x9x2-inch baking pan. Cut warm gingerbread into squares; top with dollops of the topping mixture. Sprinkle with chopped walnuts. Makes 9 servings.

SPRING GARDEN DINNER

Salisbury Steak
Asparagus-Tomato Duet
Tossed Salad
Poppy Seed Rolls   *Butter*
Strawberry Compote
Tea   *Milk*

Basic Four Food Value of Menu (see page 5): 1 serving meat, 3 servings vegetable-fruit, 1 serving bread-cereal, and 1½ servings milk.

Special Helps: Asparagus-Tomato Duet calls for fresh asparagus—one of the bounties of spring from about February to June (the rest of the year substitute frozen or canned). To select fresh asparagus, choose stalks that look crisp and fresh with tips that are well formed and tightly closed. Avoid those with more than a few inches of light-colored woody base. Store in the refrigerator with the stem ends wrapped in moist paper toweling and the stalks sealed tightly in a container or plastic bag. When you are ready to prepare the asparagus, wash the stalks and scrape off the scales. Remove the woody base by breaking, not cutting (the stalk will snap where the tender part starts). The vegetable is now ready, so proceed with the Asparagus-Tomato Duet recipe.

STRAWBERRY COMPOTE

A triple strawberry treat—

    1 quart fresh strawberries, halved
    1 pint strawberry ice cream
    1 8-ounce carton strawberry yogurt
       (1 cup)

Spoon fresh strawberries in a large compote or individual sherbets. Stir ice cream just to soften, fold in yogurt. Drizzle ice cream mixture over fresh berries. Serves 6 to 8.

SALISBURY STEAK

Mushrooms enhance the brown gravy—

  1½ pounds ground beef
    2 tablespoons grated onion
    1 teaspoon salt
    ¼ teaspoon dried marjoram leaves,
       crushed
    ⅛ teaspoon pepper
    1 envelope brown gravy mix
    1 3-ounce can sliced mushrooms,
       drained
    3 tablespoons dry red wine
       (optional)

Combine ground beef, grated onion, salt, marjoram, and pepper; mix well. Divide meat into six portions; shape into oval patties about ¾ inch thick. Broil ground beef patties 3 inches from the heat for 4 to 5 minutes. Turn and broil 3 to 4 minutes longer for medium-done meat. Remove patties to a hot platter.

Meanwhile, prepare gravy mix according to package directions. Stir in mushrooms and wine, if desired. Heat through. Pour gravy over meat patties. Garnish with sprigs of parsley, if desired. Makes 6 servings.

ASPARAGUS-TOMATO DUET

    3 slices bacon
    ¼ cup sliced green onion
    3 tablespoons vinegar
    1 tablespoon water
    2 teaspoons sugar
    ¼ teaspoon salt
            • • •
  1½ pounds fresh asparagus, bias-cut
       in 1½-inch pieces (3 cups)
    2 medium tomatoes, cut in wedges

Cook bacon till crisp; drain, reserving drippings. Crumble bacon and set aside. Add onion to reserved drippings; cook till tender. Add crumbled bacon, vinegar, water, sugar, and salt. Bring to boiling; add asparagus. Cover and cook 5 minutes. Add tomato wedges; cover and cook till heated through, about 3 minutes, spooning liquid over often. Serves 6.

Menus for Entertaining

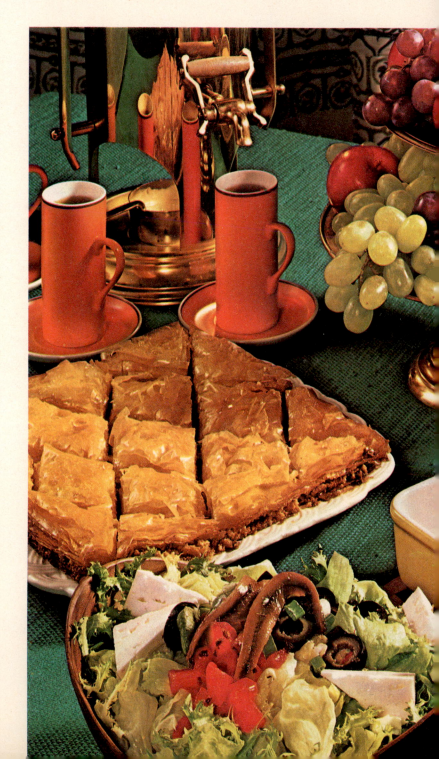

Mediterranean mood

Invite armchair travelers on a culinary cruise of the Mediterranean. Then, choose a menu centered around the foods of Greek origin. Begin with delicate *Lemon Soup* and follow it with *Greek Salad* characterized by black olives, anchovies, and feta cheese. *Pastitsio* is the main-course casserole of meat, pasta, tomatoes, and a smooth, custard topping. For dessert, arrange a bowl of fresh fruit and set out a platter of *Baklava*. Turkish coffee finishes the meal. (Recipes on page 48.)

Knowing which foods go together in preparation time as well as in eye appeal and flavor is the trademark of a successful partygiver. Acquire this know-how by using one of the menus in this chapter for your next dinner party, informal buffet, or holiday gathering. The recipes and special helps with each menu are designed to assist you in serving memorable food and to give you extra time with your guests.

INFORMAL DINNERS
AND BUFFETS

```
┌─────────────────────────────┐
│                             │
│        PATIO PARTY          │
│                             │
│         Sangria             │
│   Curried Beef Rib Roast    │
│  Zucchini-Tomato Skillet    │
│     Bibb Lettuce Salad      │
│  Fantan Rolls      Chutney  │
│   Fresh Fruit in Melon Bowl │
│                             │
└─────────────────────────────┘
```

Basic Four Food Value of Menu (see page 5): 1 serving meat, 3 servings vegetable-fruit, 1 serving bread-cereal, and no servings milk.

Special Helps: The cooking time for a rotisserie roast is affected by the diameter of the meat. Therefore, use the suggested roasting time in the recipe only as a guide for when to put the meat on the rotisserie. Determine doneness by periodically checking internal temperature with a roast meat thermometer placed in the center of the thickest part of the meat.

If you prefer to cook the Curried Beef Rib Roast in the oven, place the meat on a rack in a shallow pan and roast, uncovered, at 325°.

SANGRIA

Cut outer peel from 1 orange into long spiral strip without membrane; place in 2-quart container. Squeeze orange and 1 lemon; add to peel. Slice 1 unpeeled lemon into thin cartwheels. Add to juice with 2 bottles rosé, *or* Burgundy, *or* other red wine (4/5 quart per bottle); ½ cup sugar; and 3 tablespoons brandy (2 jiggers). Stir to dissolve sugar. Chill. Pour into punch bowl or into two pitchers. Add 1 quart chilled sparkling water. Makes 2 quarts.

CURRIED BEEF RIB ROAST

½ cup long grain rice
¼ cup dry sherry
1 beef bouillon cube, crumbled
1 tablespoon curry powder
1 tablespoon snipped parsley
1 clove garlic, minced
½ teaspoon turmeric
⅛ teaspoon freshly ground pepper
1 5-pound boned, rolled beef rib roast

In saucepan bring ¾ cup water, rice, sherry, and bouillon to boiling. Reduce heat; simmer till rice is tender, about 15 minutes. Make a paste of curry, parsley, garlic, turmeric, pepper, and 1 tablespoon water. Carefully unroll roast; rub all surfaces with curry mixture. Spread rice on unrolled surface. Reroll roast; tie securely. Balance on spit. Roast over medium coals till meat thermometer reads 145° for medium-rare, about 3 hours. (This allows for a 5° rise in temperature while meat rests before carving.) For well-done beef take meat from spit at 165°. Makes 8 to 10 servings.

ZUCCHINI-TOMATO SKILLET

½ cup green onion, sliced
1 clove garlic, minced
1 teaspoon salad oil
1 teaspoon sugar
1 bay leaf
2 pounds unpeeled zucchini, sliced ½ inch thick (6 cups)
3 peeled tomatoes, cut in eighths

Cook onion and garlic in oil till tender. Add sugar, bay leaf, 1 teaspoon salt, ⅛ teaspoon pepper, and zucchini. Cover; simmer 10 minutes, stirring occasionally. Add tomatoes; heat. Remove bay leaf. Serves 10 to 12.

A pungent curry rub on all surfaces plus a tantalizing rice stuffing rolled right with the meat are the gourmet cook's special secrets to preparing a *Curried Beef Rib Roast.*

MEDITERRANEAN DINNER

(pictured on page 44)

Lemon Soup
Pastitsio
Greek Salad
Hard Rolls   *Butter*
Baklava   *Fruit*
Red Wine   *Turkish Coffee*

Basic Four Food Value of Menu (see page 5): 1 serving meat, 2 servings vegetable-fruit, 1¼ servings bread-cereal, and ¼ serving milk.

Special Helps: This party menu lends itself either to buffet service or to a progressive dinner. In the latter plan the soup course is the first stop. Use mugs if sit-down space is limited. At the next location the salad and Pastitsio (pah seet′si o) are accompanied by rolls and red wine. The Baklava (bah′kluh vah′), fruit, and Turkish coffee are served at the final stop.
• Before baking the Pastitisio, sprinkle it with cinnamon. The spice complements the flavors in this luscious main dish.
• Frozen phyllo pastry for the Baklava is sold at Greek grocery stores or other markets that feature international foods.

LEMON SOUP

2 10½-ounce cans condensed
    chicken-rice soup
1 10½-ounce can condensed chicken
    broth
¼ cup lemon juice
3 well-beaten eggs

In a large saucepan combine soup, broth, 3 cups water, and lemon juice; bring to boil. Gradually stir some of the hot soup mixture into eggs. Return to saucepan. Cook and stir over low heat till slightly thickened, 2 to 3 minutes. Don't boil. Serve at once. Serves 12.

GREEK SALAD

1 medium head iceberg lettuce,
    chopped (6 cups)
1 head curly endive, chopped
2 tomatoes, peeled and chopped
¼ cup pitted ripe olives, sliced
¼ cup sliced green onion
⅔ cup olive or salad oil
⅛ cup white wine vinegar
½ teaspoon salt
¼ teaspoon dried oregano leaves,
    crushed
⅛ teaspoon pepper
3 ounces feta cheese, cubed
    (¾ cup)
1 3-ounce can anchovy fillets,
    drained

Toss greens in large bowl or arrange on individual plates. Arrange tomato, olives, and green onion atop greens. In screw-top jar combine olive oil, vinegar, salt, oregano, and pepper. Cover; shake well. Pour over salad. Top with feta cheese and anchovies. Serves 12.

BAKLAVA

1 pound package frozen phyllo pastry
1 cup butter, melted
½ pound walnuts *or* blanched
    almonds, finely chopped (2 cups)
½ cup sugar
½ teaspoon ground cinnamon
¾ cup sugar
¾ cup honey
1 cup water
1 tablespoon lemon juice

Thaw pastry and separate sheets. Place *half* in a greased 15x10x1-inch baking pan, brushing each with some of the melted butter. Combine nuts, ½ cup sugar, and cinnamon; sprinkle evenly over buttered pastry. Place remaining sheets on top, brushing each with melted butter. Cut into 2-inch diamonds. Bake at 400° till brown and crisp, 30 to 35 minutes. Meanwhile, bring remaining ingredients to boiling; boil till syrupy, 20 minutes. Cool. Pour over pastry. Makes 45 pieces.

Salad lovers relish the olive oil- and vinegar-dressed combination of greens, black olives, onions, anchovies, tomatoes, and feta cheese that make up *Greek Salad*.

PASTITSIO

1½ pounds ground beef
 1 medium onion, chopped (1 cup)
 1 16-ounce can tomatoes, cut up
 1 6-ounce can tomato paste
 1 teaspoon salt
 ¼ teaspoon dried thyme leaves,
    crushed
 1 7-ounce package elbow macaroni
 4 slightly beaten egg whites
 2 ounces feta cheese *or* process
    American cheese, cubed (½ cup)
 ½ cup butter or margarine
 ½ cup all-purpose flour
 1 teaspoon salt
 ¼ teaspoon ground cinnamon
 4 cups milk
 4 slightly beaten egg yolks

Cook beef and onion in skillet till meat is browned; drain excess fat. Add tomatoes, tomato paste, 1 teaspoon salt, and thyme. Simmer, covered, 30 minutes, stirring occasionally.

Meanwhile, cook macaroni according to package directions; drain. Stir egg whites and cheese into drained macaroni; add meat mixture. Put in 13½x8¾x1¾-inch baking dish.

In large saucepan melt butter or margarine. Blend in flour, 1 teaspoon salt, and cinnamon. Add milk all at once. Cook and stir till thickened and bubbly. Remove from heat. Gradually stir some of the white sauce into egg yolks; blend well. Return yolk mixture to white sauce, stirring rapidly. Pour over meat mixture in baking dish. Sprinkle lightly with additional cinnamon. Bake at 375° till heated through, 35 to 40 minutes. Let stand 10 minutes before serving. Makes 12 servings.

APPETIZER BUFFET

Spicy Meatballs   Cocktail Franks
Shrimp Canapés
Cheese-Olive Spread or *Sombrero Dip*
Assorted Crackers
Topaz Punch   Mixed Drinks

Basic Four Food Value of Menu (see page 5): All food groups are included. No amounts are given since this is not a meal and since each guest will pick a different combination.

Special Helps: The menu above is designed for 30 persons. If there are less than 30 guests, eliminate either the Shrimp Canapés or the Cocktail Franks. If the group is larger, serve Cheese-Olive Spread and Sombrero Dip.

Guests may choose mixed drinks or punch. Since the cherry-studded sherbet ring contains some of the punch ingredients, it decorates, cools, and flavors the punch all during the serving time. The bubbly, nonalcoholic grape juice gives the punch a special tingle. (If you omit the cocktails, double the punch recipe.)

SOMBRERO DIP

  ½ pound ground beef
  ½ cup chopped onion
  ¼ cup extra-hot catsup
  ½ teaspoon chili powder
  ½ teaspoon salt
  1 8-ounce can undrained red kidney
     beans
  2 ounces sharp process American
     cheese, shredded (½ cup)
     Corn chips

Cook meat and ¼ *cup* onion till meat is brown. Stir in catsup, chili powder, and salt. Add beans; mash mixture well. Heat through. Top with cheese and remaining onion. Keep warm in chafing dish. Pass corn chips. Makes 2 cups.

TOPAZ PUNCH

  ½ cup red maraschino cherries
  ½ cup green maraschino cherries
  1 quart lemon sherbet
  1 6-ounce can frozen lemonade
     concentrate, thawed (⅔ cup)
  1 6-ounce can frozen orange juice
     concentrate, thawed (⅔ cup)
  1 quart water
  ¼ cup sugar
  2 bottles sparkling catawba juice
     (25 ounces each)

To prepare sherbet ring, arrange red and green cherries in bottom of a 5-cup ring mold. Stir lemon sherbet to soften; spoon into mold over cherries, pressing to make firm ring. Freeze several hours or overnight.

In large bowl or pitcher combine fruit, concentrates, and water; stir till blended. Add sugar and stir till dissolved. Chill.

At serving time dip sherbet mold in hot water; invert and unmold ring into empty punch bowl. Pour in chilled juice mixture. Resting rim of bottle on edge of bowl, slowly pour catawba juice into punch bowl. Mix gently to blend with fruit mixture. Makes 20 five-ounce servings.

SPICY MEATBALLS

  ¾ pound ground beef
  1 4¾-ounce can liver spread
  1 teaspoon prepared mustard
  ½ teaspoon salt
  ⅛ teaspoon pepper
  ¼ cup fine dry bread crumbs
  1 slightly beaten egg
  2 cups corn chips, crushed (¾ cup)

Combine beef, liver spread, mustard, salt, and pepper till well blended. Add crumbs and egg; mix thoroughly. Shape into 1-inch balls, using one rounded teaspoon meat mixture for each. Cover tightly and refrigerate overnight. Just before baking, roll in crushed corn chips. Bake on rack in shallow pan at 350° for 10 minutes; turn once and bake 10 minutes more. Transfer to chafing dish or other heated tray to keep hot during serving time. Makes 60 meatballs.

CHEESE-OLIVE SPREAD

1 8-ounce package cream cheese,
   softened
1 6-ounce package smoky cheese roll,
   softened
¼ cup sliced pimiento-stuffed green
   olives

Line a 2-cup bowl or mold with clear plastic wrap. Beat cheeses together till blended; stir in olives. Turn into mold. Chill overnight. Turn out of mold; peel off wrap and smooth the surface. Garnish with olives, if desired.

COCKTAIL FRANKS

Since they are purchased fully cooked, cocktail franks need only a quick heating. Place franks in saucepan and cover with cold water. Bring to boiling; remove from heat. Drain and transfer to heated serving tray or chafing dish.

SHRIMP CANAPÉS

1 large cucumber
2 cups chopped, cooked shrimp
½ cup mayonnaise or salad dressing
1 tablespoon lemon juice
2 teaspoons finely chopped onion
¼ teaspoon salt
16 slices firm-textured bread
   Parsley

Wash unpeeled cucumber thoroughly; cut in half lengthwise. With a spoon, scoop out seeds from center of each section. Chop enough cucumber to make 1 cup. Save remaining cucumber to slice and use for a garnish. Combine chopped cucumber, shrimp, mayonnaise, lemon juice, onion, and salt. Chill.

Shortly before serving, trim the crusts from the bread and toast the slices. Spread shrimp mixture on toast. Cut each toast slice into 4 triangles. Garnish with parsley or a twist of cucumber. Makes 64 small sandwiches.

As guests gather around the appetizer table, offer both hot and cold tidbits. Include *Spicy Meatballs, Cocktail Franks, Shrimp Canapés,* and a smoky *Cheese-Olive Spread.*

FIESTA DINNER

Margarita Cocktails   Citrus Starter
Rio Grande Pork Roast
Buttered Asparagus Spears
Bean-Avocado Salad   Sliced Tomatoes
Corn Breadsticks   Butter
Coffee Ice Cream
Coffee

Basic Four Food Value of Menu (see page 5):
1 serving meat; 4 servings vegetable-fruit, 1 serving bread-cereal, and ½ serving milk.

Special Helps: Serve Margarita Cocktails in salt-rimmed cocktail glasses prepared by rubbing the rim of the glass with a piece of fresh lime, then by dipping the rim in salt. You can do the same for the small glasses or punch cups to be used for the Citrus Starter.

• To ensure that the pork roast is juicy, yet well done, cook it to an internal temperature of 170° as indicated on a meat thermometer with bulb in center of thickest part of roast.

MARGARITA COCKTAIL

Put ⅔ jigger tequila, dash Triple Sec, juice of ½ lime, and ½ cup crushed ice in blender. Blend to mix; strain into glass. Makes 1 drink.

CITRUS STARTER

    2 6-ounce cans limeade concentrate
    4 cups grapefruit juice, chilled
    3 to 4 dashes bitters
    1 quart sparkling water, chilled
      Cracked ice

In a large punch bowl combine limeade concentrate, grapefruit juice, and bitters. Add sparkling water and ice. Serve in salt-rimmed glasses, if desired. Makes 2½ quarts.

RIO GRANDE PORK ROAST

    1 4-pound boneless rolled pork loin
      roast
    ½ teaspoon salt
    ½ teaspoon garlic salt
    ½ teaspoon chili powder
    ½ cup apple jelly
    ½ cup catsup
    1 tablespoon vinegar
    ½ teaspoon chili powder
    1 cup crushed corn chips

Place pork, fat side up, on rack in shallow roasting pan. Mix salt, garlic salt, and ½ teaspoon chili powder; rub into meat. Roast at 325° till meat thermometer reads 165°, about 2 to 2½ hours. In saucepan bring jelly, catsup, vinegar, and remaining chili powder to a boil. Reduce heat; simmer, uncovered, for 2 minutes. Brush on roast; sprinkle with corn chips. Continue roasting till thermometer reads 170°, about 10 to 15 minutes. Remove from oven. Let stand 10 minutes. Measure pan drippings including corn chips. Add water to make 1 cup. Heat to boiling; pass with meat. Serves 8 to 10.

BEAN-AVOCADO SALAD

    2 16-ounce cans kidney beans
    1 15-ounce can garbanzo beans
    ¼ cup sliced green onion
    ½ cup salad oil
    ¼ cup vinegar
    ¼ cup lemon juice
    2 tablespoons sugar
    ¾ teaspoon chili powder
    ½ teaspoon salt
    ⅛ teaspoon garlic salt
    ⅛ teaspoon pepper
      Lettuce
    3 to 4 avocados, halved lengthwise
      and seeded, or sliced

Drain beans; toss with onion in large bowl. Mix oil, vinegar, lemon juice, sugar, chili powder, salt, garlic salt, and pepper; pour over beans. Chill. Arrange lettuce on platter or plates; place avocados on lettuce. Spoon bean salad over avocados. Serves 8 to 10.

Rio Grande Pork Roast boasts a Southwest-style chili-seasoned sauce made with corn chips. The two kinds of beans in *Bean-Avocado Salad* reflect the region, also.

SOPHISTICATED SUPPER

(as pictured on page 4)

Steaks Bertrand
Baby Lima Beans
Salad Bowl   Creamy Garlic Dressing
Poppy Seed Rolls   Butter
Grasshopper Dessert
Red Wine   Coffee

Basic Four Food Value of Menu (see page 5): 1 serving meat, 2 servings vegetable-fruit, 1 serving bread-cereal, and ¼ serving milk.

Special Helps: Because many of the above recipes can be prepared ahead of time, this menu is a good one to serve after an event, such as a play or concert, or when a working hostess wants to give a midweek dinner party.

After-theater party—Make the Grasshopper Dessert and the Creamy Garlic Dressing earlier in the day. At the same time wash, wrap, and refrigerate the salad ingredients. Before going to the theater, arrange the salad bowl, cover it with damp paper toweling, and refrigerate it. Place the steaks in a plastic bag and marinate them in the refrigerator. At home after the performance is over, cook the beans, heat the rolls, make the coffee, and finish preparing the Steaks Bertrand.

Midweek entertaining—Prepare dessert and salad ingredients the night before. However, after work, marinate the meat for 30 minutes at room temperature and arrange the salad bowl. At serving time cook the beans, heat the rolls, make the coffee, and finish cooking the meat.

CREAMY GARLIC DRESSING

In mixing bowl combine 1 cup bottled Italian salad dressing; 1 cup mayonnaise or salad dressing; 1 ounce natural Cheddar cheese, shredded (¼ cup); and 1 teaspoon anchovy paste. Beat till mixed. Chill. Makes 2 cups.

STEAKS BERTRAND

6 beef minute steaks
⅔ cup dry red wine
1 6-ounce can whole mushrooms, drained
¼ cup snipped parsley
   Dash garlic powder
6 tablespoons butter or margarine
3 slices process Swiss cheese, halved

Place steaks in clear plastic bag; set in deep bowl. Combine wine, mushrooms, parsley, and garlic powder; pour over meat. Close bag, eliminating as much air as possible. Marinate 30 minutes at room temperature or 2 hours in the refrigerator. Drain meat, reserving marinade.

In large skillet melt butter. Quickly cook *half* of the meat in the butter, about 2 minutes on each side. Remove meat to blazer pan of chafing dish; keep warm. Cook remaining meat in skillet and transfer to blazer pan. Add marinade to skillet and bring to boiling; pour over meat. Place cheese slices atop meat. Cover and place on chafing dish stand; cook over low heat till cheese melts, about 2 minutes. Serve sauce in pan with meat. Serves 6.

GRASSHOPPER DESSERT

1 cup chocolate wafer crumbs
   (about 16 cookies)
¼ cup butter or margarine, melted
1 7-ounce jar marshmallow creme
2 tablespoons crème de menthe
2 tablespoons white crème de cacao
   Few drops green food coloring
   (optional)
1 cup whipping cream

Reserve 1 tablespoon cookie crumbs. Toss remaining crumbs with melted butter. Press over bottom of an 8x8x2-inch baking pan. In small mixing bowl combine marshmallow creme, crème de menthe, crème de cacao, and food coloring. Whip till fluffy. Whip cream; fold into marshmallow mixture. Spoon into pan. Sprinkle reserved crumbs over top. Freeze 8 hours or overnight. Cut in squares. Serves 9.

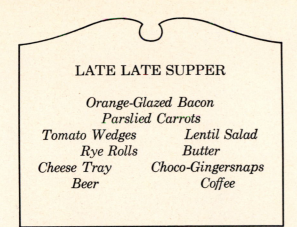

LATE LATE SUPPER

Orange-Glazed Bacon
Parslied Carrots
Tomato Wedges   Lentil Salad
Rye Rolls   Butter
Cheese Tray   Choco-Gingersnaps
Beer   Coffee

Basic Four Food Value of Menu (see page 5): 2 servings meat, 2 servings vegetable-fruit, 1 serving bread-cereal, and ½ serving milk.

Special Helps: Not all suppers are scheduled for the dinner hour. In fact, on weekends or holidays they may be as early as 5 p.m. or as late as midnight, depending on what activities are planned. This menu adapts easily.
• Buy the Canadian-style bacon unsliced, then cut it into the desired 12 slices. This allows two nice pieces per serving.
• Choose small carrots if possible and cook them whole when preparing Parslied Carrots. Otherwise, slice larger carrots with a crinkle cutter or cut into julienne strips to give them an interesting shape.

ORANGE-GLAZED BACON

  1 pound Canadian-style bacon,
      sliced in 12 pieces
  3 orange slices, quartered
 ¼ cup brown sugar
 ¼ cup orange juice
  2 tablespoons butter or margarine
  2 teaspoons lemon juice

Arrange Canadian-style bacon in an 11¾x 7½x1¾-inch baking dish; top with quartered orange slices. Combine remaining ingredients in small saucepan. Heat and stir just to boiling. Pour evenly over bacon slices. Bake, uncovered, at 375° till heated through, about 20 minutes; baste frequently with glaze. Makes 6 servings.

LENTIL SALAD

1½ cups dried lentils
  1 medium onion, sliced
 ½ teaspoon salt
  1 bay leaf

      • • •

 ½ cup chopped celery
  3 tablespoons chopped dill pickle
  2 tablespoons sliced green onion
 ⅓ cup Italian salad dressing
     Lettuce
     Snipped parsley
     Tomato wedges

In large saucepan cover the lentils with water. Add onion, salt, and bay leaf. Simmer, covered, till lentils are tender, about 45 minutes. Remove the bay leaf. Drain and cool.

Toss cooked lentils with celery, pickle, and green onion. Toss with Italian salad dressing. Chill the mixture 4 to 5 hours. Serve on lettuce. Sprinkle with snipped parsley. Garnish with tomato wedges. Makes 6 servings.

CHOCO-GINGERSNAPS

 ¾ cup shortening
  1 cup brown sugar
  1 egg
 ¼ cup molasses
2¼ cups sifted all-purpose flour
  2 teaspoons soda
  1 teaspoon ground ginger
  1 teaspoon ground cinnamon
 ½ teaspoon salt
 ¼ teaspoon ground cloves
  1 cup finely chopped almonds
  4 dozen milk chocolate candies

Cream shortening, sugar, egg, and molasses till fluffy. Sift together flour, soda, ginger, cinnamon, salt, and cloves. Stir into molasses mixture. Form into 1¼-inch balls. Roll in chopped almonds. Place 2 inches apart on greased cookie sheet. Make an indentation in top of each cookie; press in one chocolate candy, point side up. Bake at 375° for 12 minutes. Remove from pan to cooling rack immediately. Makes 4 dozen cookies.

SIT-DOWN DINNERS

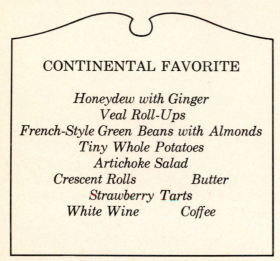

CONTINENTAL FAVORITE

Honeydew with Ginger
Veal Roll-Ups
French-Style Green Beans with Almonds
Tiny Whole Potatoes
Artichoke Salad
Crescent Rolls   Butter
Strawberry Tarts
White Wine   Coffee

Basic Four Food Value of Menu (see page 5):
1 serving meat, 4 servings vegetable-fruit, 1
serving bread-cereal, and ½ serving milk.

Special Helps: A wedge of melon such as
honeydew, cantaloupe, or Persian is a particularly good first course for a sit-down dinner.
Advance preparation is minimal, and the melon can be in place when the guests are seated.

Honeydew with Ginger is an elegant, yet
simple way to serve melon. Pass a cut-glass
shaker or antique salt dish filled with ground
ginger, and let each guest sprinkle the surface
of the melon lightly with the ginger.

● Americans are used to serving the salad
course ahead of or with the entrée. However, in
a European setting or at very formal dinners
the salad is presented after the entrée. It comes
before the cheese course, if there is one, and the
dessert. You might consider using the continental order of serving for this menu.

● The Veal Roll-Ups are a baked version of the
classic Veal Cordon Bleu that can be prepared
easily by the hostess who is also the chef and
who wishes to spend time out of the kitchen
greeting her guests. Although the sauce in the
recipe shown contains a small amount of the
same wine served with dinner, you can substitute milk for the wine when preparing it.

VEAL ROLL-UPS

1½ to 1¾ pounds veal round steak
    or cutlets, cut ¼ inch thick
6 slices thin boiled ham
3 slices process Swiss cheese
1 slightly beaten egg
2 tablespoons milk
¾ cup fine dry bread crumbs
    • • •
1 10½-ounce can condensed cream of
    mushroom soup
½ cup milk
2 tablespoons dry white wine
    Paprika

Cut veal into 6 pieces. Pound each to ⅛-inch
thickness. Top each piece with a ham slice. Cut
each cheese slice into 4 strips; place 2 on each
ham slice. Roll meat around cheese; secure
with wooden picks. Mix egg and 2 tablespoons
milk. Dip rolls in egg, then in crumbs. Place,
seam side down, in 13x9x2-inch baking dish.

Combine soup, ½ cup milk, and white wine.
Heat till bubbly; pour around rolls. Cover baking dish with foil; bake at 350° till meat is tender, about 1 hour. Uncover; sprinkle with paprika. Bake 10 minutes more to brown crumbs.
Transfer rolls to heated serving platter. Spoon
sauce on top of rolls. Makes 6 servings.

ARTICHOKE SALAD

In saucepan bring to boiling ½ cup olive oil
or salad oil; ⅓ cup vinegar; 2 tablespoons water; 4 thin slices onion; 1 tablespoon sugar; 1
clove garlic, crushed; ½ teaspoon salt; ¼ teaspoon celery seed; and dash pepper. Add one
9-ounce package frozen artichoke hearts; cook
till tender, 3 to 5 minutes. Chill thoroughly.

At serving time, drain artichokes, reserving
dressing. Combine artichokes with 4 cups torn
Bibb lettuce and 8 cherry tomatoes, halved.
Toss with enough reserved dressing to coat
salad greens. Makes 6 servings.

Cheese-filled *Veal Roll-Ups* lend a continental flair to dining. Continue the theme with piquant *Artichoke Salad* in which the marinade doubles as dressing for the salad.

CELEBRATION DINNER

Sherried Onion Soup
Ham Steak   Rye Stuffing Balls
Parslied New Potatoes   Broccoli
Crisp Relishes   Berry Sherbet Salad
Fruit-Topped Custard
or
Chocolate Marble Cake
Coffee   Tea

Basic Four Food Value of Menu (see page 5): 1 serving meat, 3 servings vegetable-fruit, 1 serving bread-cereal, and ½ serving milk.

Special Helps: When buying a Ham Steak (also known as a center-cut ham slice) to serve six, ask the meatman to cut a ham slice 1½ inches thick that will weigh around 2 pounds.

About 40 minutes before serving time, place the ham steak on a rack in an open roasting pan and bake at 325° for 20 minutes. Arrange the Rye Stuffing Balls on the rack around the ham. Bake 20 minutes longer. Stuffing balls will be cooked and ham will be heated through.

RYE STUFFING BALLS

  ¼ cup finely chopped onion
  3 tablespoons butter or margarine
  1 beaten egg
  2 teaspoons prepared mustard
  ½ teaspoon caraway seed
  6 cups fresh, light rye bread
     cubes (9 slices)

In small saucepan cook onion in butter till tender but not brown. In large bowl combine egg, mustard, caraway seed, and onion mixture. Add rye bread cubes; toss till well mixed. Shape stuffing into balls, using about ½ cup mixture for each. Arrange stuffing balls around ham steak in roasting pan and bake, uncovered, at 325° for 20 minutes. Makes 6 servings.

SHERRIED ONION SOUP

  2 10½-ounce cans condensed onion
     soup
  ½ cup dry sherry
     French bread, sliced and toasted
     Grated Parmesan cheese

Heat soup and 1½ cups water to boiling. Simmer 15 minutes. Stir in sherry. Spoon into bowls. Place a toast slice in each bowl. Sprinkle with cheese. Serves 6 to 8.

PARSLIED NEW POTATOES

  1½ to 2 pounds tiny new potatoes
  ¼ cup butter or margarine
  ¼ cup snipped parsley
  1 tablespoon lemon juice

Scrub or scrape potatoes. Cook in boiling, salted water just till tender, 15 to 20 minutes; drain. Peel potatoes, if desired. Melt butter in saucepan; stir in parsley and lemon juice. Pour over hot potatoes. Makes 6 servings.

FRUIT-TOPPED CUSTARD

  1½ cups milk
  1 3-ounce package no-bake
     custard mix
  2 tablespoons sugar
  1 8-ounce package cream cheese,
     cubed
  ½ teaspoon grated orange peel
  ⅔ cup orange juice
  2 teaspoons cornstarch
  1 cup sliced bananas and orange
     sections

In saucepan combine milk, custard mix, and sugar; add cream cheese and peel. Cook, stirring constantly, till mixture is thickened and bubbly. Remove from heat; beat with rotary beater till smooth. Pour into six ½-cup molds. Chill till set. Blend orange juice and cornstarch; cook and stir till thickened and clear. Cook 1 minute more. Cool; stir in fruit. Unmold custard; spoon on fruit sauce. Makes 6 servings.

CHOCOLATE MARBLE CAKE

2¼ cups sifted cake flour
1½ cups sugar
3 teaspoons baking powder
1 teaspoon salt
½ cup salad oil
7 egg yolks
¾ cup cold water
1 teaspoon vanilla
7 egg whites
½ teaspoon cream of tartar
¼ cup boiling water
2 tablespoons sugar
2 1-ounce squares unsweetened
chocolate, melted

Sift flour, sugar, baking powder, and salt into mixing bowl. Make a well in center of dry ingredients and add in order the oil, egg yolks, cold water, and vanilla. Beat till smooth. In another bowl beat egg whites and cream of tartar till very stiff peaks form. Pour yolk mixture in thin stream over entire surface of egg whites, gently folding to blend. Remove *one-third* of batter to another bowl. Blend boiling water, sugar, and chocolate; fold into smaller portion of batter. Spoon half the light batter into an ungreased 10-inch tube pan; top with half the chocolate batter. Repeat layers. With narrow spatula swirl gently through batters to marble. Bake at 325° about 65 minutes. Invert; cool. Frost the cake with Choco-Cream Frosting.

CHOCO-CREAM FROSTING

1 6-ounce package semisweet
chocolate pieces (1 cup)
¼ cup butter or margarine
½ cup dairy sour cream
1 teaspoon vanilla
¼ teaspoon salt
2½ to 2¾ cups sifted confectioners'
sugar

Melt chocolate and butter over hot, not boiling water. Remove from hot water; stir in sour cream, vanilla, and salt. Slowly beat in confectioners' sugar till desired spreading consistency. Spread on Chocolate Marble Cake.

BERRY SHERBET SALAD

2 3-ounce packages *or* 1 6-ounce
package raspberry-flavored
gelatin
1½ cups boiling water
1 pint raspberry sherbet
1 tablespoon lemon juice
1 16-ounce can whole cranberry
sauce
Lettuce leaves

Dissolve raspberry-flavored gelatin in boiling water; stir in sherbet and lemon juice. Chill, if necessary, till mixture mounds. Mash cranberry sauce slightly with fork; fold into gelatin mixture. Turn mixture into a 5½-cup ring mold; chill. Unmold onto lettuce-lined plate. Pass mayonnaise, if desired. Serves 8.

A velvety, cream cheese custard is the make-ahead base for *Fruit-Topped Custard*, a refreshing finale to a company dinner.

Let the host show his carving skill by cutting meaty slices from roast leg of *Lamb with Pineapple*. Use sprigs of mint, watercress, or parsley to dress up the platter.

SUNDAY DINNER SPECIAL

Vegetable Juice Frost
Lamb with Pineapple
Twice-Baked Potatoes   Peas with Mint
Romaine Lettuce Salad
Parker House Rolls   Butter
Easy Chocolate Torte
Milk   Tea

Basic Four Food Value of Menu (see page 5): 1 serving meat, 4 servings vegetable-fruit, 1½ servings bread-cereal, and 1 serving milk.

Special Helps: For something a little out of the ordinary, serve vegetable juice as an ice. To prepare Vegetable Juice Frost, stir 1 tablespoon lemon juice and ¼ teaspoon bottled hot pepper sauce into 6 cups canned vegetable juice cocktail. Pour the mixture into freezer trays; freeze. Remove from the freezer 15 minutes before serving. Spoon into sherbet glasses and garnish with lemon slices.

• To carve a leg of lamb, place the meat with shank end at the carver's right. (Cut a few slices from the bottom and wedge them underneath to steady roast.) Starting at the shank end, cut out a small wedge. Cut slices perpendicular to the horizontal leg bone. Release slices by running knife along leg bone, starting at the shank end. Turn the roast on its side and cut additional slices.

PEAS WITH MINT

    2 10-ounce packages frozen peas
    ¼ cup sliced green onions
    ¼ cup butter or margarine, melted
    ¼ teaspoon dried mint leaves

Cook peas according to package directions; drain. In small skillet cook onions in butter till tender but not brown. Add onion and mint to peas. Heat through. Makes 8 servings.

LAMB WITH PINEAPPLE

    1 6-pound frenched leg of lamb
    2 teaspoons salt
       Dash pepper
    1 20-ounce can sliced pineapple
    ¼ cup sugar
    1 tablespoon cornstarch
       Dash salt
    1 slightly beaten egg yolk
    2 tablespoons butter or margarine

Rub leg of lamb with salt and pepper. Place meat, fat side up, on rack in shallow roasting pan. Roast, uncovered, at 325° till meat thermometer registers 175°, about 3 hours.

Meanwhile, drain pineapple, reserving syrup. Add water to syrup to equal 1 cup liquid. Combine sugar, cornstarch, and salt. Add liquid and cook and stir till thickened. Stir a small amount of hot mixture into egg yolk. Return egg to hot mixture; cook 1 minute. Stir in butter or margarine. Arrange 3 to 4 pineapple slices on lamb; spoon on sauce to glaze. Roast 10 minutes longer. Cut remaining pineapple slices into chunks; add to sauce. Pass with meat. Makes 10 to 12 servings.

EASY CHOCOLATE TORTE

    1 6-ounce package semisweet
       chocolate pieces (1 cup)
    ¼ cup boiling water
    ½ cup butter or margarine,
       softened
    ¼ cup confectioners' sugar
    2 egg yolks
    1 teaspoon vanilla
    1 unsliced pound cake

Place chocolate pieces and boiling water in blender container. Blend till chocolate is dissolved. Add butter, confectioners' sugar, egg yolks, and vanilla. Blend till smooth. (Stop blender; scrape sides once or twice.) Chill frosting till it reaches spreading consistency.

Slice pound cake crosswise into 5 layers. Spread chocolate frosting between layers and over top of the cake. Chill till serving time. Makes 10 to 12 servings.

HOLIDAY DINNER

Grapefruit Grenadine
Roast Turkey   Oyster Stuffing
Mashed Potatoes   Gravy
Rutabaga and Apple Bake
Herbed Green Beans
Crisp Relishes   Cranberry Sauce
Butterhorn Rolls   Butter
Tutti-Fruitcake
Coffee   Milk

Basic Four Food Value of Menu (see page 5): 1 serving meat, 5 servings vegetable-fruit, 2 servings bread-cereal, and 1 serving milk.

Special Helps: The suggested appetizer, Grapefruit Grenadine, is made by draining the slightly sweetened juice from chilled white grapefruit sections, either canned or fresh, and by tinting the juice a rosy hue with one or more teaspoonfuls of grenadine syrup. How much grenadine you use is a matter of preference. Serve grapefruit and syrup in sherbet glasses.
• The open-pan roasting method is the secret to serving a beautifully browned turkey that carves easily and has a rich flavor. You will notice that the foil is only placed over the bird, not closed tightly around it. Thus, the heat circulates around the turkey as it roasts. This promotes even browning and prevents the less-appealing steamed flavor that develops when turkeys are tightly covered.

A roast meat thermometer is an easy-to-use means of testing doneness of a turkey. You can also use the "pinch test." Be sure to protect your fingers with several thicknesses of paper toweling, and pinch the thickest part of the drumstick. The drumstick should feel soft and should move easily in the socket.
• In many kitchens, Rutabaga and Apple Bake will have to share the 325° oven with the turkey. Be sure to add 10 to 15 minutes to the casserole baking time to be sure that the apples are done and the mixture is heated through.

ROAST TURKEY

Thaw frozen turkey. Rinse bird; pat dry. Salt inside. Stuff. Tuck drumsticks under band of skin or tie legs to tail with string.

Place bird, breast side up, on a rack in a shallow roasting pan. Rub skin with salad oil. If meat thermometer is used, insert it into the thickest part of the thigh muscle, making sure the bulb does not touch the bone. When turkey is done, meat thermometer will read 185°.

Cover loosely with foil. Roast at 325°, using the following roasting times as a guide:
3½ to 4 hours for a 6- to 8-pound turkey;
4 to 4½ hours for an 8- to 12-pound turkey;
4½ to 5½ hours for a 12- to 16-pound turkey;
5½ to 6½ hours for a 16- to 20-pound turkey.

During the last 45 minutes, cut band of skin or string holding legs and tail. Lift off foil and continue roasting till turkey is done. Let stand 15 to 20 minutes before carving.

TUTTI-FRUITCAKE

    1 6-ounce can frozen orange juice
          concentrate, thawed
    ½ cup light molasses
    3 cups raisins
    2 cups mixed candied fruits and
          peels
    ½ cup butter or margarine
    ⅔ cup sugar
    3 eggs
    1¼ cups sifted all-purpose flour
    ¼ teaspoon baking soda
    1 teaspoon ground cinnamon
    ½ teaspoon ground nutmeg
    ¼ teaspoon ground cloves
    ¼ teaspoon ground allspice
    ½ cup chopped walnuts

Bring concentrate, molasses, and raisins to boiling. Reduce heat; simmer 5 minutes. Stir in candied fruits; set aside. Cream butter and sugar. Beat in eggs one at a time. Sift together flour, soda, and spices; stir into creamed mixture. Add fruit mixture and nuts. Turn into a greased and floured 8½-inch fluted tube pan. Bake at 275° for 2 to 2½ hours. Cool ½ hour; remove from pan. Wrap and refrigerate.

OYSTER STUFFING

In a skillet cook 1 bay leaf, ½ cup chopped celery, and ½ cup chopped onion in ¼ cup butter till tender but not brown. Discard the bay leaf. Transfer the vegetables to a large mixing bowl. Add 6 cups dry bread cubes and 1 tablespoon snipped parsley; mix thoroughly.

Drain 1 pint raw oysters, reserving the liquor. Chop the oysters; add to the bread cubes with 2 beaten eggs, 1 teaspoon poultry seasoning, 1 teaspoon salt, and dash pepper. Mix well. Add milk to the reserved oyster liquor to make ¼ to ⅓ cup. Add enough of the liquid to the stuffing to moisten as desired. Makes enough stuffing for a 10-pound turkey.

RUTABAGA AND APPLE BAKE

6 cups peeled rutabaga slices
2 medium unpeeled apples, cored and thinly sliced
¾ cup brown sugar
¼ cup butter or margarine
Salt

Cook rutabaga slices in boiling, salted water till just tender; drain. Place *half* the rutabaga slices and *half* the apple slices in a greased 2-quart casserole. Sprinkle with *half* the brown sugar, dot with *half* the butter, and sprinkle with salt. Repeat layers. Bake, covered, at 350° for 30 minutes Makes 10 servings.

When doing your holiday baking, include rich, fruit-filled *Tutti-Fruitcake*. Bake the cake in a tube or fluted pan, and decorate it with sprigs of holly, fruit, and a candle.

Menus from Leftovers

Delectable bonus dinner

Are you looking for a way to
use up those bits and pieces
of last night's roast? Then
serve ever-popular *Italian
Spaghetti* with a rich meat
sauce. The mildness of the
roast is a pleasant balance
for the spicy pepperoni.
As speedy complements for
the spaghetti, serve a mixed
green salad and crisp garlic
bread. Purchase spumoni,
pistachio, or a favorite
ice cream flavor for dessert.
(Recipe on page 66.)

While it is true that some leftovers are planned, others just seem to happen. Imaginative use of these problem foods turns them into many a mealtime bonus. The menus in this chapter, which feature a main-dish recipe or an accompaniment for the main dish, make good use of leftovers. Each will present common leftovers such as meat, poultry, and vegetables in uncommonly delicious new ways.

MEAT ENCORES

SPAGHETTI NIGHT

(pictured on preceding page)

Italian Spaghetti
Tossed Salad   Garlic Bread
Spumoni or Pistachio Ice Cream
Red Wine   Coffee   Milk

SANDWICH SUPPER

Pickled Meat Loaf on Rye Bread
Gazpacho Relish   Leaf Lettuce
Potato Chips
Baked Custard
Milk   Coffee

Basic Four Food Value of Menu (see page 5): 1 serving meat, 1 serving vegetable-fruit, 2 servings bread-cereal, and 1¼ servings milk.

Special Helps: Cook spaghetti "al dente" or "tender to the tooth." Some firmness remains, but the starchy taste is gone. Drain well.

ITALIAN SPAGHETTI

    2 cups water
    1 15-ounce can tomato sauce with
        mushrooms
 1½ cups finely chopped, cooked pork
    1 4-ounce package pepperoni, sliced
    3 beef bouillon cubes
  ½ cup chopped onion
  ¼ cup chopped green pepper
    2 tablespoons snipped parsley
    1 teaspoon sugar
  ½ teaspoon salt
  ½ teaspoon dried oregano leaves,
        crushed
  ½ teaspoon dried thyme leaves,
        crushed
    1 clove garlic, minced
      Cooked spaghetti

Simmer first 13 ingredients, uncovered, in a large saucepan for 45 minutes. Stir often. Spoon over spaghetti. Makes 4 or 5 servings.

Basic Four Food Value of Menu (see page 5): 1 serving meat, 1 serving vegetable-fruit, 2 servings bread-cereal, and 1¼ servings milk.

Special Helps: An open-face sandwich designed for eating with a knife and fork is often a more attractive showcase for leftover meat loaf (see the recipe on page 27) than just tucking the meat between two slices of bread. Since cooked meats are not usually colorful by themselves, add to the sandwich foods that are as appealing to the eye as they are complementary in flavor. The peppy Gazpacho Relish on one half of the sandwich is a decorative touch that doubles as salad and meat accompaniment.

GAZPACHO RELISH

    3 fresh tomatoes
  ½ cup diced green pepper
  ⅓ cup vinegar
  ¼ cup chopped onion
    1 tablespoon sugar
  ¾ teaspoon celery salt
  ¾ teaspoon mustard seed
  ¼ teaspoon salt
      Dash pepper

Peel and finely chop tomatoes. In mixing bowl combine tomatoes with remaining ingredients. Chill well to blend flavors. Makes 3 cups.

Pickled Meat Loaf on Rye Bread takes on Spanish airs when served with *Gazpacho Relish*. Fresh vegetables and bright seasonings add color and flavor to the sandwich.

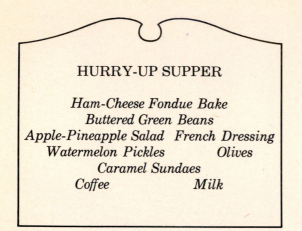

HURRY-UP SUPPER

Ham-Cheese Fondue Bake
Buttered Green Beans
Apple-Pineapple Salad   French Dressing
Watermelon Pickles   Olives
Caramel Sundaes
Coffee   Milk

Basic Four Food Value of Menu (see page 5): 2 servings meat, 2 servings vegetable-fruit, 1 serving bread-cereal, and 2 servings milk.

Special Helps: Make Apple-Pineapple Salad by alternating apple slices and pineapple rings on lettuce-lined plates. Pass dressing.

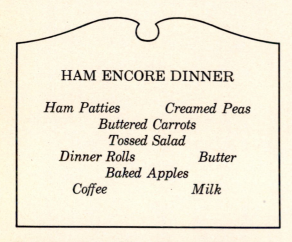

HAM ENCORE DINNER

Ham Patties   Creamed Peas
Buttered Carrots
Tossed Salad
Dinner Rolls   Butter
Baked Apples
Coffee   Milk

Basic Four Food Value of Menu (see page 5): 1 serving meat, 2½ servings vegetable-fruit, 1½ servings bread-cereal, 1½ servings milk.

Special Helps: The Ham Patties are a make-ahead main dish. Combine the ham-rice mixture several hours before needed. Chill so that the patties will hold their shape during cooking.
● At mealtime, prepare the Creamed Peas by making 1½ cups medium white sauce. Add one 10-ounce package frozen peas, cooked and drained. Spoon over the Ham Patties.

HAM-CHEESE FONDUE BAKE

  2 tablespoons butter or margarine
  ½ cup chopped onion
  5 slices bread, cut in cubes
  2 cups diced, leftover or fully
      cooked ham
  4 ounces process American cheese,
      shredded (1 cup)
  1 7½-ounce can tomatoes, drained
  3 beaten eggs
1¼ cups milk
  ⅛ teaspoon dry mustard

In small saucepan melt butter. Add onion; cook till tender but not brown. Add bread cubes, diced ham, cheese, and drained tomatoes to skillet; toss gently to mix well. Pour into an 8x8x2-inch baking dish.

Combine eggs, milk, and dry mustard. Pour over ham mixture in baking dish. Bake at 350° for 25 to 30 minutes. Makes 4 to 6 servings.

HAM PATTIES

2 cups ground fully cooked ham
1 cup cooked rice
¼ cup chopped celery
2 tablespoons chopped onion
1 tablespoon chopped green pepper
2 tablespoons shortening
2 tablespoons all-purpose flour
1 teaspoon prepared mustard
  Dash pepper
½ cup milk
1 beaten egg
½ cup fine dry bread crumbs
2 tablespoons shortening

In mixing bowl combine ham and rice. In small saucepan cook celery, onion, and green pepper in 2 tablespoons shortening till tender but not brown. Blend in flour, mustard, and pepper. Add milk; cook and stir till very thick and bubbly. Combine with ham-rice mixture. Chill.

Form ham mixture into 10 patties. Dip each in mixture of beaten egg and 1 tablespoon water; coat with bread crumbs. In large skillet cook patties in hot shortening till brown, 3 to 4 minutes on each side. Serves 4.

LOUISIANA LUNCHEON

Creole Jambalaya
(pictured on page 2)
Romaine Lettuce   Creamy Dressing
Corn Breadsticks   Butter
Pecan-Topped Sugar Cookies
Milk   Coffee

Basic Four Food Value of Menu (see page 5): 1 serving meat, 2 servings vegetable-fruit, 2 servings bread-cereal, and 1 serving milk.

Special Helps: The Creole Jambalaya not only stretches leftover ham in a delectable main dish, but it also makes the most of a small amount of cooked shrimp. If you have access to a market where fresh shrimp is available, you can cook and shell 12 ounces of raw shrimp to equal the amounts called for in this recipe.

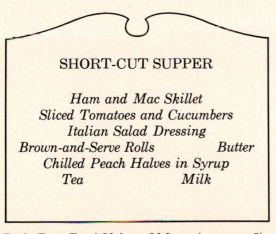

SHORT-CUT SUPPER

Ham and Mac Skillet
Sliced Tomatoes and Cucumbers
Italian Salad Dressing
Brown-and-Serve Rolls   Butter
Chilled Peach Halves in Syrup
Tea   Milk

Basic Four Food Value of Menu (see page 5): 1 serving meat, 2½ servings vegetable-fruit, 2 servings bread-cereal, and 1 serving milk.

Special Helps: You can prepare this meal in 20 minutes. Slice the vegetables, brown the rolls, put peaches in serving bowl, and even boil water for the tea while the skillet dish cooks.

CREOLE JAMBALAYA

¾ cup chopped onion
1 clove garlic, minced
2 tablespoons butter or margarine
1 28-ounce can tomatoes, cut up
1 10½-ounce can condensed beef
　broth
1 cup uncooked long grain rice
1 bay leaf, crushed
1 teaspoon sugar
½ teaspoon dried thyme leaves,
　crushed
¼ teaspoon chili powder
2 cups cubed, leftover ham
7 or 8 ounces frozen shelled shrimp,
　cooked and cut in half, *or* one
　4½-ounce can shrimp, drained
¼ cup sliced pitted ripe olives
1 green pepper, cut in 1-inch pieces

Cook onion and garlic in butter till tender. Add next 7 ingredients and 1 cup water. Simmer, covered, till rice is tender, about 15 minutes. Add remaining ingredients; simmer, uncovered, 5 to 10 minutes. Serves 6 to 8.

HAM AND MAC SKILLET

2 cups water
½ cup sliced celery
¼ cup chopped onion
¼ cup chopped green pepper
1 chicken bouillon cube
½ teaspoon dry mustard
1 7½-ounce package macaroni and
　cheese dinner mix
½ cup milk
2 cups cubed, leftover or fully
　cooked ham

In skillet combine water, celery, onion, green pepper, bouillon cube, dry mustard, and the *macaroni portion* of the macaroni and cheese dinner mix. Cover skillet. Cook, stirring occasionally, till macaroni is tender, about 6 to 7 minutes. Stir in the package of cheese from dinner mix and milk. Distribute ham over the top. Cover and continue cooking till mixture is heated through, about 10 minutes. Serves 4.

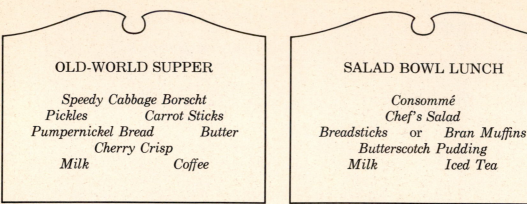

OLD-WORLD SUPPER

Speedy Cabbage Borscht
Pickles   Carrot Sticks
Pumpernickel Bread   Butter
Cherry Crisp
Milk   Coffee

SALAD BOWL LUNCH

Consommé
Chef's Salad
Breadsticks   or   Bran Muffins
Butterscotch Pudding
Milk   Iced Tea

Basic Four Food Value of Menu (see page 5): ½ serving meat, 1½ servings vegetable-fruit, 1 serving bread-cereal, and 1 serving milk.

Special Helps: Speedy Cabbage Borscht, a beetless version of an old-world favorite, is a good way to use up small pieces of leftover cooked lamb, beef, or pork.

Avoid overcooking the cabbage. Simmer the soup just until the cabbage shreds are tender, not soft. The meat needs no further cooking.

SPEEDY CABBAGE BORSCHT

A robust main dish soup—

    4 cups coarsely shredded cabbage
       (1 small head)
    1 28-ounce can tomatoes, cut up
    2 cups cubed cooked lamb, beef,
       or pork
    1 10½-ounce can condensed beef
       broth
    1 soup can water (1⅓ cups)
    1 cup chopped onion
    1 medium tart apple, peeled and
       diced
    2 tablespoons lemon juice
    1 tablespoon sugar
    1 teaspoon salt
    ¼ teaspoon pepper

In Dutch oven or large kettle combine all ingredients. Bring to boiling; reduce heat. Simmer, covered, till cabbage is tender, about 30 minutes. Ladle into soup bowls. Serves 8.

Basic Four Food Value of Menu (see page 5): 1½ servings meat, 2 servings vegetable-fruit, 1 serving bread-cereal, and 1¼ servings milk.

Special Helps: Assemble the salad in one large or four smaller bowls. Save some of the prettiest lettuce pieces to tuck around the edge.

CHEF'S SALAD

    1⅓ cups salad oil
    ½ cup vinegar
    2 small cloves garlic, minced
    2 teaspoons sugar
    1½ teaspoons salt
    1½ teaspoons dry mustard
       Dash pepper
    2 cups leftover or cooked roast beef
       cut in strips
    3 hard-cooked eggs, cut in quarters
    2 ounces Swiss cheese, cut in strips
    1½ cups cherry tomatoes, halved
    ½ cup sliced radishes
    8 cups torn lettuce

Shake first 7 ingredients in a screw-top jar. Arrange beef, eggs, cheese, tomatoes, and radishes on lettuce. Pass dressing. Serves 4.

Soup and salad teammates

Chef's Salad brings together beef, eggs, cheese, and vegetables in a peppy dressing. Hot consommé is a flavor complement.

HOLIDAY SEASON BRUNCH

Orange Juice
Turkey-Potato Pancakes
Cranberry Sauce   Crisp Relishes
Cheese Tray   Nuts and Mints
Coffee   Hot Cocoa

Basic Four Food Value of Menu (see page 5): 2 servings meat, 3 servings vegetable-fruit, no servings bread-cereal, and 1 serving milk.

Special Helps: You can use a blender to coarsely chop rather than shred the potatoes. Process in water in two batches. Drain well.

LADIES' CLUB LUNCHEON

Cheese Soup
Turkey-Fruit Salad
Hot Biscuits   Honey Butter
Crème de Menthe Sundaes
Coffee   Tea

Basic Four Food Value of Menu (see page 5): 1 serving meat, 2 servings vegetable-fruit, 1 serving bread-cereal, and 1 serving milk.

Special Helps: Consider the party uses of cooked turkey when you shop for the bird—a large one is often the best buy, too. After cooking, remove the leftover meat from the bones, package it in heavy foil or freezer wrap in two- or four-cup amounts, and freeze till it is your turn to entertain the club for luncheon.
• Make Honey Butter by beating ½ cup butter with an electric mixer till fluffy. Gradually add ¼ cup honey; continue beating till blended.

TURKEY-POTATO PANCAKES

  3 beaten eggs
  3 cups shredded, peeled, uncooked
      potato, drained (3 potatoes)
1½ cups finely chopped turkey
1½ teaspoons grated onion
     Dash pepper
  1 tablespoon all-purpose flour
1½ teaspoons salt
     Cranberry sauce

In mixing bowl combine eggs, shredded potato, turkey, onion, and pepper. Add flour and salt; mix well. Using about ¼ cup batter to make each pancake, drop batter onto a hot, greased griddle. With a spatula, spread pancake to about 4 inches in diameter. Cook over medium-low heat till potato is done, about 3 to 4 minutes on each side. Serve hot with warmed cranberry sauce. Makes about 15 pancakes.

TURKEY-FRUIT SALAD

  2 medium oranges
  4 cups cubed, cooked or leftover
      turkey
     Salt
     Pepper
  1 cup sliced celery
  1 8¾-ounce can pineapple tidbits,
      drained
 ½ cup mayonnaise or salad dressing
  1 teaspoon sugar
 ½ teaspoon dry mustard
 ⅛ teaspoon salt
  6 lettuce cups

Peel the oranges, removing as much of the white membrane as possible. Section and then dice the oranges over a bowl to catch the juice. Season the turkey generously with salt and pepper. Combine the diced oranges, turkey, celery, and pineapple. Cover and chill the mixture. Combine mayonnaise, 1 tablespoon of the orange juice, sugar, dry mustard, and the ⅛ teaspoon salt; blend thoroughly. Cover and chill. Just before serving, lightly toss the turkey-fruit mixture with dressing; serve the salad in lettuce cups. Makes 6 servings.

CASSEROLE NIGHT

Chicken-Cheese Bake
Buttered Green Beans
Tossed Salad
Sliced Oranges   Pumpkin Cookies
Coffee   Milk

Basic Four Food Value of Menu (see page 5): 2 servings meat, 3 servings vegetable-fruit, ½ serving bread-cereal, and 1½ servings milk.

Special Helps: Canned green chilies come in several degrees of hotness. When buying them for the Chicken-Cheese Bake, be sure to read the label on the can so that you get the one that suits your family's taste preferences. If you want a milder casserole, use 2 instead of 3 tablespoons chilies in the recipe.

Crisp corn chips wreathe *Chicken-Cheese Bake*, a creamy mixture that gets added pep from chopped green chilies.

PUMPKIN COOKIES

    1 cup shortening
    1 cup sugar
    1 cup canned pumpkin
    1 egg
    1 teaspoon vanilla
    2 cups sifted all-purpose flour
    1 teaspoon baking powder
    ½ teaspoon baking soda
    ½ teaspoon salt
    1 teaspoon ground cinnamon
    ½ teaspoon ground nutmeg
    ¼ teaspoon ground allspice
    1 cup raisins
    ½ cup chopped nuts

Cream shortening and sugar. Add pumpkin, egg, and vanilla; beat well. Sift together flour, baking powder, soda, salt, and spices. Add to creamed mixture; blend well. Stir in raisins and nuts. Drop by rounded teaspoons, 2 inches apart, on greased cookie sheet. Bake at 350° for 12 to 15 minutes. Makes 3½ dozen cookies.

CHICKEN-CHEESE BAKE

Leftover turkey could replace the chicken—

    1 10½-ounce can condensed cream of
         chicken soup
    1 8-ounce jar process cheese spread
    ½ cup milk
    2 cups diced, leftover or cooked
         chicken
    3 tablespoons chopped, canned
         green chilies
    2 teaspoons instant minced onion
    4 cups corn chips

In saucepan heat together soup and cheese spread till blended. Gradually stir in milk; add chicken, chilies, and onion. Cook and stir till bubbly. Crush half of the corn ships. Place in 1½-quart casserole. Pour in soup mixture; top with remaining chips. Bake at 350° for 20 minutes. Let stand 5 minutes. Serves 4 or 5.

MENU STRETCHERS

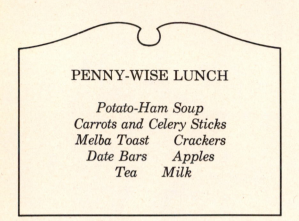

PENNY-WISE LUNCH

Potato-Ham Soup
Carrots and Celery Sticks
Melba Toast   Crackers
Date Bars   Apples
Tea   Milk

Basic Four Food Value of Menu (see page 5): ½ serving meat, 3 servings vegetable-fruit, 1½ servings bread-cereal, and 1½ servings milk.

Special Helps: Use this menu for an economical box lunch. The soup stays hot in a vacuum bottle, and the crisp vegetables, crackers, date bars, and apple rate high in totability.

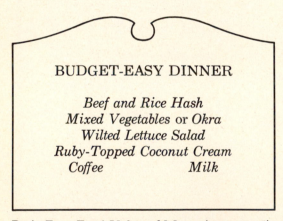

BUDGET-EASY DINNER

Beef and Rice Hash
Mixed Vegetables or Okra
Wilted Lettuce Salad
Ruby-Topped Coconut Cream
Coffee   Milk

Basic Four Food Value of Menu (see page 5): 1 serving meat, 3 servings vegetable-fruit, 1 serving bread-cereal, and 1½ servings milk.

Special Helps: When making Ruby-Topped Coconut Cream, fold 1 cup coconut into prepared vanilla pudding. Top each serving with a spoonful of red jelly. Serve with milk.

POTATO-HAM SOUP

Turn those extra mashed potatoes into a quick, hot soup for lunch or supper—

- ¼ cup chopped celery
- 2 tablespoons chopped onion
- 2 teaspoons snipped chives
- 2 tablespoons butter or margarine
- 2 cups milk
- 1½ cups mashed potatoes
- 1 chicken bouillon cube
- 1 cup finely diced, leftover or fully cooked ham

In a large saucepan cook celery, onion, and chives in butter or margarine till tender but not brown. Add milk, mashed potatoes, and chicken bouillon cube; blend together till smooth. Stir in ham. Bring the soup mixture *almost* to boiling; reduce heat and simmer 20 minutes, stirring occasionally. Makes 4 servings.

BEEF AND RICE HASH

Cook too much rice yesterday? Team it with ground beef for today's hearty main dish—

- 1 pound ground beef
- ½ cup chopped onion
- ⅓ cup chopped green pepper
- 1 16-ounce can tomatoes, cut up
- 2 cups cooked rice
- 1 tablespoon chili sauce
- ¾ teaspoon salt
- ⅛ teaspoon pepper
- 2 ounces process American cheese, shredded (½ cup)

In skillet cook ground beef, onion, and green pepper till meat is browned and vegetables are tender. Drain off fat. Stir in tomatoes, rice, chili sauce, salt, and pepper. Cover and simmer 10 minutes. Sprinkle cheese over hash; cover and cook till cheese has melted. Serves 4.

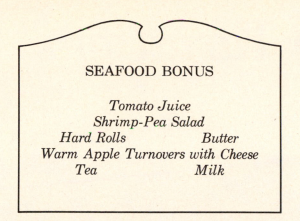

SEAFOOD BONUS

Tomato Juice
Shrimp-Pea Salad
Hard Rolls   Butter
Warm Apple Turnovers with Cheese
Tea   Milk

Basic Four Food Value of Menu (see page 5): 1 serving meat, 3 servings vegetable-fruit, 1½ servings bread-cereal, and 1 serving milk.

Special Helps: Although the peas and shrimp get top billing in the salad, preparation of the lettuce is important, too. Tearing the greens into bite-sized pieces rather than cutting them with a knife is recommended. The torn edges expose the juicy interior and allow the dressing to be absorbed more readily.

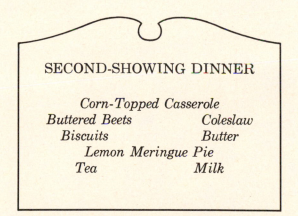

SECOND-SHOWING DINNER

Corn-Topped Casserole
Buttered Beets   Coleslaw
Biscuits   Butter
Lemon Meringue Pie
Tea   Milk

Basic Four Food Value of Menu (see page 5): 1 serving meat, 2½ servings vegetable-fruit, 1¼ servings bread-cereal, and 1 serving milk.

Special Helps: Use leftover vegetables such as corn to top casseroles. The splash of color is particularly welcome with creamed mixtures. Before adding the topping, be sure the mixture in the baking dish is hot so that the vegetables do not dry out from prolonged heating.

SHRIMP-PEA SALAD

Use the peas left from last night's dinner with canned shrimp in tonight's main course salad—

    2 cups cooked peas
    1 4½-ounce can shrimp, drained
    ⅓ cup sliced pitted ripe olives
    ⅓ cup salad oil
    3 tablespoons vinegar
    ½ teaspoon salt
    ⅛ teaspoon dried dillweed, crushed
      Dash pepper
    3 to 4 cups torn lettuce
    2 hard-cooked eggs, sliced

In bowl combine peas, shrimp, and olives. In screw-top jar combine oil, vinegar, salt, dillweed, and pepper; shake well. Pour dressing over mixture in bowl. Cover and refrigerate several hours. Drain shrimp-pea mixture; reserve dressing. Arrange lettuce in a salad bowl. Top with shrimp-pea mixture. Toss with just enough of the reserved dressing to moisten. Garnish salad with egg slices. Makes 4 servings.

CORN-TOPPED CASSEROLE

Present leftover corn and beef in a new guise—

    2 cups cubed, leftover or cooked beef
    ¼ cup sliced green onion
    2 tablespoons salad oil
    1 10½-ounce can condensed cream
      of celery soup
    ¼ cup milk
    1 cup leftover whole kernel corn
    1 slightly beaten egg
    ¼ cup cracker crumbs
    2 tablespoons chopped canned
      pimiento
    1 tablespoon snipped parsley
    1 tablespoon butter or margarine,
      melted

Brown the beef and onion in hot oil. Stir in soup and milk. Heat through. Spoon meat mixture into a 1-quart baking dish. Combine remaining ingredients. Spoon over meat mixture. Bake at 350° for 15 to 20 minutes. Serves 4.

Menus with Variations

Changing menu plans

Give *Marinated Rump Roast* (on page 20) a completely new set of menu partners. Prepare tender lima beans, buttered noodles, and a shimmering molded salad to accompany the flavorful, juicy meat. For dessert, bake a spice cake in square pans and frost it with caramel frosting. Serve glasses of milk or mugs of hot coffee as beverages.

Selecting a menu can be difficult if you have family members who dislike having the same menu for favorite foods or who have vegetable likes and dislikes. To help you overcome this, select from the alternate menus—there's one for each main dish in this book—or recipes—there are extra recipes for the most popular vegetables, which can be switched from one menu to another—in this chapter.

MENU ALTERNATES

Each main dish in the preceding chapters is included here in a different menu. Many of the vegetables, salads, and desserts are in new combinations, too. (Recipe page numbers are indicated.) Menus also have been built around favorites such as chili, macaroni and cheese, or pot roast. Recipes for some of the foods accompanying them are keyed to this book.

MAIN DISH	ACCOMPANIMENTS	SALAD	BREAD	DESSERT
BAKED HAM	Potato-Cheese Custard (see page 91) buttered broccoli spears	cranberry and celery salad mold	crescent rolls and butter	chocolate fondue with bananas, apples, marshmallows, and angel cake for dippers
BEEF AND RICE HASH (see page 74)	buttered whole green beans	lettuce wedges with green goddess dressing	whole wheat bread and butter	Slice-O-Lemon Pudding (see page 20) or apples and peanut butter cookies
BEEF-CABBAGE CASSEROLE (see page 37)	carrot sticks	molded fruit salad (made with low-calorie gelatin)	rye bread and butter	plain sugar cookies
BRAISED LIVER WITH ONIONS	au gratin potatoes	sliced tomatoes with French dressing	hard rolls and butter	Frosty Pineapple Pie (see page 21) or deep-dish fruit pie
BROILED STEAKS OR CHOPS	Crisp Dilled Celery (see page 90) or Zesty Fiesta Corn (see page 91)	tossed salad and Creamy Garlic Dressing (see page 54)	hot rolls and butter	strawberry shortcake
CHEF'S SALAD (see page 70)	hot spiced cranberry juice cocktail—served as an appetizer		Melba toast and butter	warm upside-down cake
CHICKEN CACCIATORE (see page 23)	Italian green beans	sliced cucumbers and onion rings in sour cream	hard rolls and butter	lemon sherbet with crème de menthe syrup topping
CHICKEN CASSEROLE	baked acorn squash halves	tomato aspic or molded vegetable salad with mayonnaise	garlic toast	Fruit à la Mode (see page 32)
CHICKEN CHASSEUR (see page 18)	asparagus spears	tossed salad with blue cheese dressing	dinner rolls and butter	Berry Cheesecake Pie (see page 26)

MAIN DISH	ACCOMPANIMENTS	SALAD	BREAD	DESSERT
CHICKEN-CHEESE BAKE (see page 73)	buttered baby lima beans *or* peas	apple wedges and sliced celery on lettuce with French dressing	hot biscuits and butter	lime sherbet
CHILI	grapefruit juice— served as an appetizer	celery, carrots, chili peppers, and pickles on a relish tray	corn bread and butter	ice cream and Choco-Gingersnaps (see page 55)
CORN-TOPPED CASSEROLE (see page 75)	stewed tomatoes *or* Harvard beets	cheese-stuffed celery sticks	whole wheat rolls and butter	banana-nut cake with buttercream frosting
CRANBERRY PORK CHOPS (see page 41)	buttered noodles and whole green beans	Garden Salad (see page 25)	bread and butter	Pumpkin Cookies (see page 73)
CREOLE JAMBALAYA (see page 69)		tossed green salad with French dressing	French rolls and butter	Easy Chocolate Torte (see page 61) *or* chilled cantaloupe wedges à la mode
CURRIED BEEF RIB ROAST (see page 46)	corn on the cob with butter	marinated tomatoes and onion rings on lettuce	Vienna bread and butter	Fruit à la Mode (see page 32)
FRANKFURTERS	tomato soup and Swiss cheese	Vegetable-Dill Combo (see page 34)	toasted buns and butter	rice pudding
FRIED CHICKEN	Polka-Dot Beans (see page 84) and boiled small potatoes	tossed vegetable salad with green goddess dressing	popovers *or* bread and butter	Marshmallow Ice Cream (see page 35) and lemon cookies *or* apricot tarts
GLAZED CORNED BEEF (see page 29)	Parslied New Potatoes (see page 58) and mixed vegetables	Guacamole Salad— served as appetizer (see page 28)—and celery sticks	hard rolls and butter	lime sherbet
GRILLED PORK CHOPS	Skillet Cabbage (see page 89) *or* Creamy Lima Beans (see page 88)	orange slices and onion rings on lettuce	pumpernickel bread and butter	raisin pie *or* oatmeal cookies
HAM AND MAC SKILLET (see page 69)	buttered spinach	cherry tomatoes, celery, and radishes on a relish tray		Chocolate Marble Cake (see page 59) *or* chocolate layer cake

MAIN DISH	ACCOMPANIMENTS	SALAD	BREAD	DESSERT
HAMBURGERS	potato chips	Greek Salad (see page 48) *or* tossed green salad with Italian dressing	toasted buns with Horseradish Butter (see page 35)	baked custard
HAM-CHEESE FONDUE BAKE (see page 68)	Dilled Peas (see page 84) *or* buttered asparagus	tossed salad and Italian dressing	hard rolls and butter (optional)	brownies with chocolate frosting
HAM PATTIES (see page 68) and POACHED EGGS	broiled tomato halves	celery sticks	toasted English muffins and Honey Butter (see page 72)	chilled ambrosia
HAM STEAK with RYE STUFFING BALLS (see page 58)	baked carrots and buttered French-style green beans	Artichoke Salad (see page 56)	fantan rolls and butter (optional)	Tutti-Fruitcake (see page 62)
SAUSAGE CASSEROLE (see page 42)	Brussels sprouts *or* Italian green beans	molded salad	corn bread sticks and butter	fresh nectarines *or* peaches and crisp sugar cookies
HEARTY HODGEPODGE (see page 31)		wedges of iceberg lettuce with Italian dressing *or* French dressing	breadsticks and butter	Applesauced Gingerbread (see page 42) *or* ice cream sundaes
HOME-STYLE ROUND STEAK (see page 26)	baked potatoes and buttered green beans	tossed salad with blue cheese dressing	hot buttermilk biscuits and butter	brownie squares topped with scoops of vanilla ice cream and a raspberry sauce
HOT BARBECUE RIBS (see page 34)	Zucchini-Tomato Skillet (see page 46) *or* baked beans	citrus salad	Boston brown bread and butter	banana cream pie *or* butterscotch brownies
ITALIAN SPAGHETTI (see page 66)	buttered zucchini slices	romaine lettuce with Creamy Garlic Dressing (see page 54)	rye bread and butter	chilled canned pears with chocolate syrup
LAMB WITH PINEAPPLE (see page 61)	baked sweet potatoes and buttered French-style green beans	individual molded vegetable salads on lettuce	poppy seed rolls and butter	angel food cake
LENTIL SALAD (see page 55)	apple juice—served as an appetizer—and Scalloped Squash (see page 21)	radish rosettes and ripe olives	Anadama Bread (see page 29)	hot gingerbread with lemon sauce

MAIN DISH	ACCOMPANIMENTS	SALAD	BREAD	DESSERT
LIME-BASTED CHICKEN (see page 37)	Peas with Mint (see page 61)	pineapple rings with low-calorie mayonnaise-type dressing and shredded cheese	rye rolls and butter	angel food cake
LUNCHEON SPECIAL (see page 12)	buttered whole beets *or* spiced apple rings	mixed green salad with French dressing	spoon bread (part of main dish recipe)	blueberry turnovers
MACARONI AND CHEESE	buttered spinach	molded vegetable salad with mayonnaise	hard rolls and butter	Rhubarb Kuchen (see page 24) with cream
MARINATED RUMP ROAST (see page 20)	buttered noodles and baby lima beans	olive perfection salad	fantan rolls and butter	spice cake with caramel frosting
MEATBALLS	poppy seed noodles and Mapled Apple-Carrot Dish (see page 84)	combination salad and Thousand Island dressing	bread and butter (optional)	fresh blueberries *or* strawberries topped with sour cream and brown sugar
MEAT LOAF	Spinach-Rice Surprise (see page 87)	sliced tomatoes on lettuce with French dressing	toasted slices of French bread and butter	Slice-O-Lemon Pudding (see page 20)
MINUTE STEAKS	Blue Cheese-Sauced Beans (see page 86) and hashed brown potatoes	Gazpacho Relish in lettuce cups (see page 66)	toast triangles and butter	prune whip
ORANGE-GLAZED BACON (see page 55)	French-style green beans and buttered whole kernel corn	Date-Apple Waldorf (see page 25)	sesame seed rolls and butter	cream puffs filled with vanilla ice cream and topped with rum-flavored chocolate syrup
OVEN-BARBECUED TROUT (see page 21)	Peas Italian (see page 84)	cucumber and onions marinated in vinegar	Italian bread and butter	caramel custard
OVEN STEW (see page 24)	French-Style Peas (see page 84) *or* buttered broccoli and wild rice	Caesar salad	hot rolls and butter	baked apples with cream
PARMESAN OMELET and CHEDDAR CHEESE SAUCE (see page 14)	Asparagus-Tomato Duet (see page 43) *or* buttered peas	carrot curls, radish rosettes, and celery sticks	breadsticks and butter	chilled purple plums in syrup and macaroons

MAIN DISH	ACCOMPANIMENTS	SALAD	BREAD	DESSERT
PASTITSIO (see page 49)	pan-fried eggplant	assorted fresh vegetable tray	poppy seed rolls and butter	lemon sherbet and date bars
PICKLED MEAT LOAF (see page 27)	baked potatoes and buttered leaf spinach	deviled eggs and carrot curls	hard rolls and butter	peach cobbler with whipped dessert topping *or* cream
PORK ROAST	glazed acorn squash rings and buttered baby lima beans	sliced cranberry sauce on lettuce leaves	sesame seed rolls and butter	Grasshopper Dessert (see page 54) *or* vanilla pudding
POTATO-HAM SOUP (see page 74)		lettuce wedges and French dressing	Easy Breadsticks (see page 15) and butter	pound cake with fruit topping *or* fresh raspberries
POT ROAST	potatoes and onions (cooked with the roast)	carrot and raisin salad	hot French bread and butter	Choco-Mint Cups (see page 40)
RIO GRANDE PORK ROAST (see page 52)	buttered rice *or* hominy and buttered Italian green beans	Coleslaw (see page 42)	hot rolls and butter	fresh fruit and cheese (Cheddar, Gouda, or Edam)
ROAST TURKEY (not stuffed)	Cream-Sauced Broccoli (see page 86) and baked sweet potatoes	carrot and pineapple salad mold	butterflake rolls and butter	pecan pie *or* cheesecake
ROAST TURKEY with OYSTER STUFFING (see pages 62-63)	French-Style Peas (see page 84)	ambrosia salad	Parker House rolls and butter	pumpkin pie *or* lime sherbet
SALISBURY STEAK (see page 43)	Carrots Au Gratin (see page 90)	peach halves on lettuce topped with cottage cheese	cloverleaf rolls and butter	vanilla ice cream and Praline Sauce (see page 28)
SHRIMP-PEA SALAD (see page 75)	Citrus Starter (see page 52)—served as an appetizer	tomato wedges	hot muffins and butter	Berry Cheesecake Pie (see page 26)
SHRIMP-VEGETABLE DINNER (see page 38)		molded fruit salad (made with low-calorie gelatin)	warmed Chinese noodles	orange sherbet and vanilla wafers
SPEEDY CABBAGE BORSCHT (see page 70)		pear half with cream cheese balls rolled in chopped nuts topped with French dressing	bagels and butter	Slice-O-Lemon Pudding (see page 20)

MAIN DISH	ACCOMPANIMENTS	SALAD	BREAD	DESSERT
STEAKS BERTRAND (see page 54)	French Onion Casserole (see page 88) and buttered zucchini slices	relish tray	hot rolls and butter	orange chiffon cake
STUFFED PEPPERS	Beets with Raisins (see page 89)	Fresh Fruit Salad (see page 36) and Berry Dressing (see page 37)	breadsticks and butter	Easy Chocolate Torte (see page 61) *or* coconut cake
TACO-SEASONED STEAK (see page 32)	Pimiento-Creamed Corn (see page 91) and buttered whole okra	Hot Bean Salad (see page 29) *or* tossed salad with vinegar and oil dressing	garlic bread warmed on the grill	ice cream with pineapple topping
TOMATO-SAUCED FISH (see page 40)	hashed brown potatoes and buttered peas	combination salad and Italian dressing	butterflake rolls and butter	jelly roll
TOSTADO CASSEROLE (see page 28)	Spinach Patties (see page 87) *or* cauliflower	tossed salad with choice of dressings	hot corn bread and butter	assorted fresh fruit *or* melon ball compote
TUNA CASSEROLE	Tarragon Beets (see page 89) *or* buttered whole kernel corn	raw spinach tossed salad	Salty Breadsticks (see page 15) *or* hot bran muffins and butter	cherry pie
TUNA-RICE SALAD (see page 15)		relish tray	Toasted slices of Sourdough Bread (see page 31) *or* French bread	Fruit-Topped Custard (see page 58)
TURKEY-FRUIT SALAD (see page 72)	cream of mushroom soup *or* onion soup and assorted crackers —served as an appetizer	olives and pickles	cinnamon toast	Peanut Brittle Cookies (see page 17)
TURKEY-POTATO PANCAKES (see page 72)	Bacon-Flavored Beans (see page 86) *or* Polka-Dot Beans (see page 84)	spicy applesauce		fruitcake
VEAL ROLL-UPS (see page 56)	buttered asparagus spears	slices of fresh fruit (peaches, apples, plums, or pears) with yogurt dressing	French rolls and butter	Grasshopper Dessert (see page 54)

SUBSTITUTE RECIPES

MAPLED APPLE-CARROT DISH

  1 large onion, sliced (about ¾ cup)
  3 tablespoons butter or margarine
  6 medium carrots, peeled and sliced
  2 tablespoons maple-flavored syrup
  ½ teaspoon salt
  2 medium unpeeled tart apples, cut
      in wedges

Cook onion in butter till tender but not brown. Add carrots, syrup, and salt; cover and cook over low heat for 15 minutes. Add apple; cover and simmer till carrots are tender, about 15 minutes more. Stir occasionally. Serves 6.

DILLED PEAS

  ¼ cup water
  2 beef bouillon cubes
  3 tablespoons butter or margarine
  1 teaspoon instant minced onion
  ¼ teaspoon dried dillweed, crushed
      Dash pepper
  2 10-ounce packages frozen peas

In saucepan bring water to boiling. Blend in bouillon cubes, butter, onion, dillweed, and pepper. Add peas. Return to boiling and simmer till tender, about 5 minutes. Serves 6.

PEAS ITALIAN

  1 10-ounce package frozen peas
  1 tablespoon salad oil
  ⅓ cup finely diced fully cooked ham
  2 tablespoons chopped green onion
  ¼ teaspoon dried basil leaves,
      crushed

Cook peas according to package directions; drain. Heat oil in skillet. Add ham, onion, and basil. Cook, stirring often, for 5 minutes; toss with peas. Makes 3 or 4 servings.

FRENCH-STYLE PEAS

  ¼ cup sliced green onion
  2 tablespoons butter or margarine
  2 cups shelled fresh peas or
      1 10-ounce package frozen peas
  1 tablespoon water
  1 teaspoon dried chervil leaves,
      crushed
  ½ teaspoon sugar
  ½ teaspoon salt
      Dash pepper
  1 cup torn iceberg lettuce
  1 tablespoon snipped parsley

Cook onion in butter till tender. Add peas, water, chervil, sugar, salt, and pepper. Cook, covered, till peas are tender—5 minutes for frozen and 8 to 15 minutes for fresh. Stir in lettuce; cook just till lettuce is wilted, 1 minute. Sprinkle with parsley. Serves 4.

POLKA-DOT BEANS

  2 tablespoons chopped onion
  2 tablespoons butter or margarine
  2 tablespoons sliced pimiento-stuffed
      green olives
  ¼ teaspoon salt
  ¼ teaspoon paprika
      Dash pepper
  1 9-ounce package frozen cut green
      beans, cooked and drained

Cook onion in butter till tender but not brown. Add olives, salt, paprika, and pepper. Toss with beans; heat through. Serves 3 or 4.

Family pleasers

Vary menus by serving vegetables in new → ways. Prepare *Polka-Dot Beans*, *Mapled Apple-Carrot Dish*, or *French-Style Peas*.

BLUE CHEESE-SAUCED BEANS

    1 9-ounce package frozen French-
         style green beans
    2 tablespoons butter or margarine
    2 tablespoons all-purpose flour
   ¼ teaspoon salt
       Dash pepper
    1 cup milk
    2 tablespoons blue cheese, crumbled
   ¼ cup fine cornflake crumbs
    1 tablespoon butter or margarine,
         melted

Cook beans according to package directions;
drain well. In saucepan melt the 2 tablespoons
butter or margarine. Blend in flour, salt, and
pepper. Add milk all at once. Cook and stir
till thickened and bubbly. Stir in blue cheese.
Pour sauce over beans. Toss cornflake crumbs
with the 1 tablespoon melted butter; sprinkle
over beans. Makes 4 servings.

BACON-FLAVORED BEANS

    2 9-ounce packages frozen cut green
         beans or 2 16-ounce cans cut
         green beans, drained
    5 slices bacon
   ¼ cup chopped green onion
         • • •
   ½ cup cold water
    1 tablespoon vinegar
    1 tablespoon cornstarch
    1 teaspoon sugar
   ¼ teaspoon salt
       Dash pepper

Cook frozen beans according to package directions; drain. In skillet cook bacon till crisp;
drain, reserving 1 tablespoon drippings. Crumble bacon; set aside. In reserved drippings
cook onion till tender but not brown.
   Combine cold water and vinegar; blend in
cornstarch. Stir cornstarch mixture, sugar,
salt, and pepper into onions in skillet. Cook
and stir till thickened and bubbly. Cook 1
minute more. Add drained beans, stirring to
coat with sauce. Heat through. Pour into serving dish; top with crumbled bacon. Serves 6.

CREAM-SAUCED BROCCOLI

*Use fresh broccoli when in season or frozen
broccoli to prepare this elegant vegetable—*

    1 pound fresh broccoli or 1 10-ounce
         package frozen broccoli spears
    1 3-ounce package cream cheese,
         cubed
   ¼ cup milk
    1 teaspoon lemon juice
   ¼ teaspoon ground ginger
   ⅛ teaspoon ground nutmeg
       Toasted slivered almonds
         (optional)

To cook fresh broccoli, first split stalk almost
to flowerets and tie in a bundle with a strip of
foil. Then, stand bundle in 1 inch of boiling,
salted water. Cover and cook till tender, 15 to
20 minutes; drain. Cook frozen broccoli according to package directions; drain.
   Meanwhile, in saucepan combine cream
cheese, milk, lemon juice, ginger, and nutmeg.
Cook and stir over low heat till blended and
hot through. Alternating heads and stalks, arrange hot broccoli on a serving dish. Pour
cream sauce over top. Garnish with almonds,
if desired. Makes 3 or 4 servings.

CREOLE-STYLE BROCCOLI

*Combine broccoli and a flavorful tomato sauce
for a unique side dish vegetable—*

    1 10-ounce package frozen chopped
         broccoli
    2 tablespoons chopped onion
    2 tablespoons butter or margarine
    1 tablespoon all-purpose flour
    1 8-ounce can tomatoes, cut up
   ½ teaspoon sugar

Cook broccoli according to package directions;
drain. Meanwhile, in a small saucepan cook
onion in butter till tender but not brown. Blend
in flour. Add tomatoes, sugar, and ½ teaspoon
salt. Cook till mixture is thickened and bubbly.
Combine broccoli and tomato mixture. Turn
into serving dish. Makes 4 servings.

SPINACH-RICE SURPRISE

        2 cups water
        ¾ cup uncooked long grain rice
        1 tablespoon instant minced onion
        1 teaspoon salt
        1 10-ounce package frozen chopped
            spinach
        4 ounces process American cheese,
            cubed (1 cup)

In covered saucepan simmer water, rice, onion, and salt for 15 minutes. Add spinach; simmer, covered, 10 minutes more. Stir occasionally. Remove from heat. Add cheese; let stand 1 to 2 minutes. Stir just to blend. Serves 6 to 8.

SPINACH PATTIES

        1 10-ounce package frozen chopped
            spinach, cooked
        2 cups soft bread crumbs (2½ slices)
        2 beaten eggs
        2 tablespoons finely chopped onion
        ¼ teaspoon salt
        ⅛ teaspoon ground nutmeg (optional)
        2 tablespoons butter or margarine

Drain spinach *thoroughly*. Combine spinach, bread crumbs, eggs, onion, salt, and nutmeg. Shape into 6 patties. Melt butter in skillet. Fry patties till brown, about 4 minutes on each side. Makes 4 to 6 servings.

SEASONING CHART FOR VEGETABLES

The addition of an herb or spice will heighten the natural flavor of a vegetable. Use about ¼ teaspoon dried herb or spice for each 4 servings. If using fresh herbs, increase the amount 3 times. Add seasonings with the salt and pepper—usually near the end of cooking (except bay leaf, which is added in the beginning).

Asparagus	caraway seed, mustard, nutmeg, sesame seed, tarragon
Beans—green	basil, dill, marjoram, mustard, nutmeg, oregano, savory, thyme
Beets	allspice, bay leaf, caraway seed, cloves, ginger, mustard
Broccoli	caraway seed, mustard, oregano, tarragon
Brussels sprouts	caraway seed, mustard, nutmeg, sage
Cabbage	caraway seed, celery seed, cumin, curry powder, fennel, mustard
Carrots	allspice, bay leaf, cinnamon, curry powder, dill, ginger
Cauliflower	cayenne, celery seed, chili powder, nutmeg, paprika, rosemary
Corn	cayenne, celery seed, chili powder, curry powder, paprika
Eggplant	allspice, bay leaf, chili powder, marjoram
Onions	bay leaf, mustard, oregano, paprika, sage
Peas	chili powder, dill, oregano, poppy seed, rosemary, sage
Potatoes	caraway seed, fennel, mustard, oregano, paprika, sesame seed
Spinach	allspice, cinnamon, nutmeg, oregano, rosemary, sesame seed
Squash	allspice, bay leaf, cinnamon, cloves, ginger, nutmeg, paprika
Sweet potatoes	cardamom seed, cinnamon, cloves, nutmeg, poppy seed
Tomatoes	basil, celery seed, chili powder, curry powder, oregano
Turnips	allspice, celery seed, curry powder, dill, oregano

CREAMY LIMA BEANS

The rich, sweet flavor comes from the sour cream and brown sugar in the sauce—

    1 10-ounce package frozen baby
        lima beans
    2 tablespoons chopped green onion
    1 tablespoon butter or margarine
    1 tablespoon all-purpose flour
    ¼ teaspoon salt
        Dash pepper
    ½ cup milk
    2 tablespoons brown sugar
    ½ cup dairy sour cream

Cook lima beans according to package directions; drain well. In medium saucepan cook green onion in butter till tender but not brown. Blend in flour, salt, and pepper. Add milk and brown sugar. Cook and stir till thickened and bubbly. Add sour cream and cooked lima beans to sauce mixture. Heat through, but do not boil. Makes 4 servings.

CURRIED ONIONS

A spicy vegetable to serve with beef or lamb at company and family dinners—

    1 pound whole small onions
    2 tablespoons butter or margarine
    2 tablespoons all-purpose flour
    ½ teaspoon salt
    ¼ teaspoon curry powder
    ¼ teaspoon paprika
    1 cup milk
    ½ cup soft bread crumbs
    1 tablespoon butter or margarine,
        melted

Peel onions; cook in boiling, salted water for 15 minutes. In saucepan melt the 2 tablespoons butter; blend in flour, salt, curry powder, and paprika. Add milk; cook and stir till thickened and bubbly. Stir in cooked onions. Turn onion mixture into a 1-quart casserole. Toss bread crumbs with the 1 tablespoon melted butter. Sprinkle over onion mixture. Bake at 350° for 35 minutes. Makes 5 or 6 servings.

FRENCH ONION CASSEROLE

    4 medium onions, sliced
    3 tablespoons butter or margarine
    2 tablespoons all-purpose flour
        Dash pepper
    ¾ cup beef bouillon
    ¼ cup dry sherry
    1½ cups plain croutons
    2 tablespoons butter or margarine,
        melted
    2 ounces process Swiss cheese,
        shredded (½ cup)
    3 tablespoons grated Parmesan
        cheese

Cook onions in the 3 tablespoons butter just till tender. Blend in flour and pepper. Add bouillon and sherry; cook and stir till thickened and bubbly. Turn into a 1-quart casserole. Toss croutons with the 2 tablespoons melted butter; spoon atop onion mixture. Sprinkle with Swiss and Parmesan cheeses. Place under broiler *just* till cheeses melt, about 1 minute. Serve immediately. Makes 4 to 6 servings.

Broiling *French Onion Casserole* briefly before serving melts the Swiss cheese and Parmesan cheese and warms the croutons.

CAULIFLOWER WITH TOMATO

Shredded American cheese sprinkled over cooked vegetables adds flavor and color—

  1 large head cauliflower
  1 8-ounce can stewed tomatoes
  ½ teaspoon celery salt
  ⅛ teaspoon pepper
     • • •
  2 ounces process American cheese,
     shredded (½ cup)

Wash head of cauliflower and break into small flowerets. In large saucepan combine stewed tomatoes, celery salt, and pepper; bring mixture to boiling. Add fresh cauliflowerets; return to boiling. Reduce heat; simmer, covered, till cauliflowerets are tender, about 15 to 20 minutes. Pour mixture into individual dishes or a serving bowl. Sprinkle with shredded cheese while warm. Makes 6 to 8 servings.

EGGPLANT-CHEESE STACKS

Serve either as a side dish vegetable for dinner or as a main dish at lunch—

  1 medium eggplant, peeled
  3 or 4 slices sharp process American
     cheese
     • • •
  1 slightly beaten egg
  ¼ cup milk
  1 2⅜-ounce package seasoned
     coating mix for chicken
  3 tablespoons salad oil

Cut peeled eggplant into six or eight ½-inch-thick slices. Cook eggplant slices, covered, in a small amount of boiling water for 2 to 3 minutes; drain well. Place a slice of process American cheese between each 2 slices eggplant; trim cheese to fit. Combine beaten egg and milk. Dip both sides of the eggplant "stacks" into the egg mixture, then dip in the seasoned coating mix for chicken.

In skillet heat salad oil; cook eggplant stacks in hot oil till golden brown, about 5 to 6 minutes on each side. Makes 4 servings.

TARRAGON BEETS

  1 16-ounce can sliced beets
  2 tablespoons butter or margarine
  1 tablespoon chopped green onion
  1 teaspoon lemon juice
  ½ teaspoon dried tarragon leaves,
     crushed
     Dash pepper

In saucepan heat beets and beet liquid; pour off beet liquid. To hot beets in saucepan add butter, onion, lemon juice, tarragon, and pepper. Cook 2 to 3 minutes more. Serves 4.

BEETS WITH RAISINS

  1 16-ounce can sliced beets
  3 tablespoons sugar
  2 teaspoons cornstarch
  ½ teaspoon ground ginger
  ¼ teaspoon salt
  1 tablespoon lemon juice
  ¼ cup raisins
  2 tablespoons butter or margarine

Drain beets, reserving ¾ cup liquid. In saucepan combine sugar, cornstarch, ginger, and salt. Blend in reserved beet liquid and lemon juice. Add raisins. Cook and stir till thickened and bubbly. Add butter and beets. Simmer till hot through, 5 to 10 minutes. Serves 4.

SKILLET CABBAGE

  ¼ cup butter or margarine
  ½ teaspoon seasoned salt
  ⅛ teaspoon ground nutmeg
  6 cups coarsely shredded cabbage
  ¼ cup chopped onion
  3 tablespoons vinegar
  2 teaspoons sugar

In large skillet melt butter; blend in seasoned salt and nutmeg. Add cabbage and onion; mix well. Cook, covered, over medium heat for 15 minutes; stir frequently. Blend vinegar and sugar. Add vinegar mixture to cabbage; toss together. Cook 5 minutes more. Makes 6 servings.

CRISP DILLED CELERY

    3 cups celery, cut ¾ inch thick
    ¼ cup chopped green pepper
    2 tablespoons chopped onion
    2 tablespoons water
    2 tablespoons butter or margarine
    1 chicken bouillon cube
    ½ teaspoon dried dillweed, crushed
    ¼ teaspoon salt

In saucepan combine all ingredients. Simmer, tightly covered, 8 to 10 minutes. Serves 6.

CREAMED CELERY

    1 chicken bouillon cube
    3 cups celery, cut ½ inch thick
    ¾ cup thinly sliced carrot
    ¼ teaspoon dried rosemary leaves, crushed
    2 tablespoons butter or margarine
    3 tablespoons all-purpose flour
    ¼ teaspoon salt
    1 cup milk

In saucepan bring ½ cup water to boiling; dissolve bouillon cube in water. Add celery, carrot, and rosemary. Simmer, covered, till tender, about 15 minutes. In another saucepan melt butter; blend in flour and salt. Add milk; cook and stir till thickened and bubbly. Stir sauce into undrained hot vegetables. Serves 6.

CARROTS AU GRATIN

    4 tablespoons butter or margarine
    ¼ cup fine saltine cracker crumbs
    2 tablespoons grated Parmesan cheese
      Dash pepper
    3 cups sliced carrots
    ¼ cup chopped green pepper
    2 tablespoons chopped onion

Melt *2 tablespoons* of the butter; toss with crumbs, Parmesan cheese, and pepper. Set aside. Cook carrots, green pepper, and onion in salted water just till tender. Drain. Stir in remaining butter. Top with crumbs. Serves 6.

SQUASH SOUFFLÉ

    3 pounds Hubbard squash
    1 cup milk
    2 tablespoons butter or margarine
    1 cup coarse, rich, round cracker
      crumbs (about 20 crackers)
    2 tablespoons finely chopped canned
      pimiento
    1 teaspoon salt
    1 teaspoon grated onion
      Dash pepper
      Dash ground nutmeg
    2 well-beaten eggs
      Strips of canned pimiento

Cut unpeeled squash into 3- to 4-inch squares. In saucepan cook squash, uncovered, in small amount of boiling, salted water till tender, 20 to 25 minutes. Remove pulp and mash (about 2 cups); discard rind. In large saucepan heat the milk and butter or margarine over low heat till butter melts. Add ¾ *cup* of the cracker crumbs; mix well. Add squash, chopped pimiento, salt, onion, pepper, and nutmeg. Stir in eggs. Pour into a 1-quart casserole: top with the remaining ¼ cup crumbs. Bake at 350° till knife inserted just off-center comes out clean, about 1 hour. Garnish with strips of pimiento, if desired. Makes 4 to 6 servings.

STUFFED ACORN SQUASH

    2 acorn squash
    1 tablespoon butter or margarine
    1 tablespoon brown sugar
    ¼ teaspoon salt
    ¼ teaspoon grated orange peel
      Orange juice
    2 tablespoons chopped pecans

Halve squash; remove seeds. Place, cut side down, on greased baking sheet. Bake at 350° till squash are tender, 30 to 35 minutes. Scoop out pulp, leaving a thin shell. Stir together squash pulp, butter, brown sugar, salt, and orange peel. Add enough orange juice (about 2 teaspoons) to make a fluffy consistency. Spoon pulp mixture into shells; sprinkle with pecans. Bake 10 minutes more. Serves 4.

BAKED CORN ON THE COB

6 ears fresh corn
1 4-ounce container whipped cream
    cheese with chives
¼ cup butter or margarine, softened
¼ teaspoon salt
    Dash pepper

Remove husks from ears of corn; remove silk with stiff brush. In small bowl stir cream cheese into butter; blend in salt and pepper. Place each ear of corn on a square of foil; spread each with a generous tablespoon of butter mixture. Fold up and seal foil. Bake at 400° till tender, about 45 minutes. Spoon hot chive butter over corn to serve. Serves 6.

PIMIENTO-CREAMED CORN

A good use for leftover corn on the cob—

1 3-ounce package cream cheese with
    pimiento, softened
¼ cup milk
1 tablespoon butter or margarine
½ teaspoon onion salt
2 cups cooked corn, cut from the cob
    (3 or 4 ears) or 1 16-ounce can
    whole kernel corn, drained

In medium saucepan combine cream cheese, milk, butter, and onion salt. Cook and stir over low heat till cheese melts. Stir in corn. Cook till corn is heated through. Serves 4 to 6.

SNAPPY BARBECUED CORN

2 10-ounce packages frozen whole
    kernel corn in butter sauce
¼ cup thinly sliced green onion
3 tablespoons bottled barbecue sauce
1 teaspoon prepared mustard

Cook corn in cooking pouch according to package directions; open pouch and turn corn into medium saucepan. Stir in onion, barbecue sauce, and mustard. Cook over medium heat, stirring occasionally, till hot through. Serves 6.

ZESTY FIESTA CORN

Goes well with roast turkey or barbecued steaks—

½ envelope taco seasoning mix
    (about 2 tablespoons)
¼ cup water
¼ cup salad oil
¼ cup vinegar
1 16-ounce can whole kernel corn,
    drained
2 medium tomatoes, peeled and
    diced (about 1½ cups)
½ cup sliced pitted ripe olives
¼ cup diced green pepper

In large bowl blend together taco seasoning mix and water; add salad oil and vinegar. Add corn, diced tomatoes, olives, and green pepper; toss lightly. Chill mixture several hours or overnight; stir occasionally. Makes 6 servings.

POTATO-CHEESE CUSTARD

2 cups diced, peeled, uncooked
    potatoes
2 cups milk
1 5-ounce jar process cheese spread
    with bacon
1 teaspoon instant minced onion

• • •

2 beaten eggs
1 tablespoon snipped parsley
½ teaspoon dry mustard
½ teaspoon salt
    Dash pepper
    Crumbled crisp-cooked bacon
    (optional)

In saucepan combine potatoes and enough water to cover; bring to boiling. Remove from heat; drain. Arrange potatoes in a 10x6x1¾-inch baking dish. Heat milk, cheese spread, and onion till cheese melts. Combine eggs, parsley, dry mustard, salt, and pepper. Gradually stir hot milk mixture into eggs; pour over potatoes. Bake at 325° till knife inserted just off-center comes out clean, 35 to 40 minutes. Top with crumbled bacon, if desired. Let stand 5 minutes before serving. Serves 6.

POTATO-ONION PUFFS

Packaged instant mashed potatoes
(enough for 4 servings)

• • •

⅓ cup packaged pancake mix
1 tablespoon dry onion soup mix
1 teaspoon finely snipped parsley

Prepare instant mashed potatoes according to package directions. Add pancake mix, dry onion soup mix, and snipped parsley. Drop potato mixture from tablespoon, a few at a time, into deep hot fat (365°). Fry till golden brown, about 1 to 1½ minutes, turning occasionally to brown all sides. Drain potato puffs on paper toweling. Serve hot. Makes 18 puffs.

CINNAMON-APPLE SWEETS

1 18-ounce can sweet potatoes, cut
in ¾-inch crosswise slices
1 8½-ounce can applesauce
2 tablespoons red cinnamon candies
3 tablespoons sugar
2 tablespoons butter or margarine,
softened
½ teaspoon salt

Place *half* of the potatoes in 1-quart casserole. Combine applesauce and candies; spread *half* of the mixture over potatoes in casserole. Repeat potato and applesauce layers. Combine sugar, butter, and salt; dot over top. Bake, covered, at 350° for 30 minutes. Serves 6.

SUBSTITUTION CHART

When you are missing a recipe ingredient, consult the chart below. You'll find a substitute that will not alter the flavor or texture of your recipe.

IN PLACE OF	SUBSTITUTE
1 cup cake flour	1 cup minus 2 tablespoons all-purpose flour
1 tablespoon cornstarch (for thickening)	2 tablespoons all-purpose flour *or* 4 teaspoons quick-cooking tapioca
1 teaspoon baking powder	¼ teaspoon baking soda plus ½ cup sour milk (to replace ½ cup of liquid in the recipe)
1 cup whole milk	½ cup evaporated milk plus ½ cup water *or* 1 cup reconstituted nonfat dry milk plus 2½ teaspoons butter or margarine
1 cup sour milk or buttermilk	1 tablespoon lemon juice or vinegar plus whole milk to make 1 cup (let stand 5 minutes)
1 whole egg (in custards)	2 egg yolks
1 1-ounce square unsweetened chocolate	3 tablespoons unsweetened cocoa powder plus 1 tablespoon butter or margarine
1 teaspoon dry mustard	1 tablespoon prepared mustard
1 cup tomato juice	½ cup tomato sauce plus ½ cup water
1 cup catsup or chili sauce (for cooked mixtures)	1 cup tomato sauce plus ½ cup sugar and 2 tablespoons vinegar
Dash bottled hot pepper sauce	Dash cayenne or red pepper

INDEX

RECIPES

A-B